PERSPECTIVE

DOROTHY LOTT

authorHOUSE®

AuthorHouse™
1663 Liberty Drive
Bloomington, IN 47403
www.authorhouse.com
Phone: 1 (800) 839-8640

Published by AuthorHouse   01/05/2016

ISBN: 978-1-5049-7038-9 (sc)
ISBN: 978-1-5049-7019-8 (e)

TABLE OF CONTENTS

FOREWORD

Poetry as defined by Webster is "writing that formulates a concentrated imaginative awareness of experience in language chosen and arranged to create a specific emotional response through meaning, sound and rhythm."

Poets have for centuries found the art form of poetry to be a great way of expressing thoughts, ideas, feelings, dreams and experiences. They try in various ways to make sense of the world in which they live through the written form of poetry.

Sometimes poems can suddenly appear out of the unexplained and unexpected. A poem can bounce around the mind through a spurt of the imagination. I often think some as appearing like pop-corn. They can start the popping process and if the lid is raised the corn (words) can fly in many directions.

The need for the process of getting it out on paper may only consist of a verse or a four line stanza as in the poem "Mr. Pennycomequick" by P. M. Stone, or it can be as long as the poem "<u>The Eve of St. Agnes</u>" by John Keats. However the end result appears... there's no doubt in the mind of the poet that the urgency of expression is all encompassing.

Reading I "The Happy Code"

"I was glad when they said unto me, let us go into the house of the Lord."

- Psalm 122:1

CRACKING THE HAPPY CODE

Happiness is pretty much decided. "I have decided to be happy."

"Don't sit around and wait for the arrival of happiness to happen. Instead, you have already happen, arise to the occasion."

Being happy may seem a small matter in the minds of some, but In the minds of others it may seem a big matter.

Happiness is trivial in the mind of an unhappy person.

"Don't exit an unhappy setting so soon; you may be the one they get happy about."

"Try being happy for one hour; and see what the other 23 will be like."

"I like to enjoy the happy in being happy."

"Imagine yourself the gift of happiness and enjoy it all year long."

A happy person may create a happy home.
A happy home may create a happy family.
A happy family may create a happy neighborhood.
A happy neighborhood may create a happy town.
A happy town may create a happy state.
A happy state may create a happy country.
A happy country may create a happy world.
Imagine a happy planet... possibilities... possibilities...possibilities.

Some may think happiness is like cracking a code to some mathematical equation. ($H_2A^3P_1P^4I_3N^5E_3S^4S_2$). Try cracking a baby code for (**GA-GA-GOO-GOO**). Can you solve the mystery? Is there one?

"When I wake up each morning... I decide to be happy."

HAPPY SCRIPTURES

"Happy art thou, O Israel: who is like unto thee, O people saved by the Lord, the shield of thy help, and who is the sword of thy excellency! and thine enemies shall be found liars unto thee; and thou shalt tread upon their high places," (Deuteronomy 33:29).

"Behold, happy is the man whom God correcteth: therefore despise not thou the chastening of the Almighty," (Job 5:17).

"For thou shalt eat the labor of thine hands: happy shalt thou be, and it shall be well with thee," (Psalm 128:2).

"Happy is that people, that is in such a case: yea, happy is that people, whose God is the Lord," (Psalm 144:15).

"She is a tree of life to them that lay hold upon her: and happy is everyone that retaineth her," (Proverbs 3:18).

"He that despiseth his neighbor sinneth: but he that hath mercy on the poor, happy is he," (Proverbs 14:21).

"Righteous art thou, O Lord, when I plead with thee: yet let me talk with thee of thy judgments: Wherefore doth the way of the wicked prosper? wherefore are all they happy that deal very treacherously?" (Jeremiah 12:1).

"And now we call the proud happy; yea, they that work wickedness are set up; yea, they that tempt God are even delivered," (Malachi 3:15).

"If ye know these things, happy are ye if ye do them," (John 13:17).

"Hast thou faith? have it to thy self before God. Happy is he that condemneth not himself in that thing which he alloweth," (Romans 14:22).

"Behold, we count them happy which endure. Ye have heard of the patience of Job, and have seen the end of the Lord; that the Lord is very pitiful, and of tender mercy," (James 5:11).

"But and if ye suffer for righteousness' sake, happy are ye: and be not afraid of their terror, neither be troubled," (1 Peter 3:14).

"Where there is no vision, the people perish: but he that keepeth the law, happy is he," (Proverbs 29:18).

THE LANGUAGE OF SMILES

Smiles are simply glorious when broken
down they reveal volumes of pretty stories,
some last only a moment, while
others linger and just want to stick around.

Many reveal the semblance of teeth –
others a closed grin.
Sometimes they break into full fledge laughter.
There are those that are just quiet and casual.

Smiles of joy announce the birth of a baby
girl or boy with lips spread far and wide.
Smiles of happiness give rise to love and marriage,
where lips never cease to rest.

Smiles of excitement break the happy scale.
Lottery winners express smiles of surprise.
While caught in the act of mischief... children
often clasp their hands and hide their smiles.

Smiles are the prettiest and purest;
as they dance around heart strings; no mistaken,
it certainly is worth the taking.

Smiles highlight genuine forms of communication,
and that's no exaggeration.
Some are destined for glamour and gold,
while most be suitable as wonders to behold.

So, give your face an astonishing smile today –
God created it to do no less than that.
Listen to the babies as they coo-coo and smile,
the angelic stuff of a million lifetimes.

IT'S HARD TO STAY DEPRESSED
STARING AT A YELLOW ROSE:

In shallowness of a bud vase –
Stood a yellow rose of extraordinary taste,
Lying between petals, oh, what
Beauty to behold,
As yellow danced around in perfect
Tune with time...
Such joy awakening...
Sparking regenerations of imaginations;
Hitting the eye, oh! Such Heavenly
Gifts of splendor,
Encapsulating dollops in a brain
Ever so gingerly,
Sending chemicals, stirring a revival...
To remind of a destiny so divine,
Awake, awake from stagnant pools
Of grey, yellow came to take you away.
She predicated her stand upon
Glitters of sun rays as they jitter
On ripples and water waived.
She stood on creation dressed in yellow
Leaves of fall. Sunflowers show off
Her dazzling brilliance each
Noon day, such an array.

The crop planted corn whistle –
In flaming winds of change
Into created fields already pre-arranged.

Egg yolk splattering protein
Against the brain;
Telling nothing is the matter
And will flatter again and again

Yellow conveniently purposed
Itself upon bars of natural gold, as

Sun from our Father's Heaven
Hits the DNA of yellow squash.
I knew lemons wore ripeness
When their yellow told me so.

Reading II "Hands"

"For thou shalt eat the labor of thine hands: happy shalt thou be, and it shall be well with thee."

- Psalm 128:2

HANDS...

The strength they hold may never be told.
Their power and complexity can rule one's destiny.
They comfort a cry as tears wipe dry.

Embraced by love causing hearts to buzz...
emphatically, I do see hands of glee...
gestures so dear my hands held near.

Every finger stands alone... each a treasure all its own...
clutching whole host of joyous life history –
repeated through pages of swirling mysteries.

They never cease to amaze the eye of their
astounding creations in a day. They have
created great paintings... built magnificent
buildings... performed heart transplants...
hugged our love ones... and thousands of blessings
that are yet untold.

God made a pair to show that He really cares.
When one is missing it really makes a difference.
The sculptor creates them artificially by the
thousands.

The master creator creates them by a mechanism
known as miracles.

So, the very next time you need an increase –
Get up, look up, and reach up... you will encounter
a hand from on high, one that created yours to
compliment His.

A POEM SPOKE TO ME

A poem spoke to me –
out of a compassion of hot pursuit –
on a day of fervent renew –
with just a slight quiver,
but in a soft and powerful voice
of shiver.

"My [P] is for Patience…
a drive to persevere after filling
a trash can full of paper on
a day when the heart just seem
out of sync with the hand."

"The [O] in me is my Overriding
desire to tell a meaningful story;
something that can be imparted in
the souls of individuals... in order
to challenge and change a life."

"The [E] in me is to Enhance a
Love relationship with the language
of poetry without always taking me
so serious; for, I can inspire
even in my moments of laughter."

"My [M] can sometimes be Mesmerizing.
It can make merry.
A joy connection to keep;
of knowing there will be another time...
another spurt of inspiration... another pen
and paper... when it will all come together
and a masterpiece is what one perceives
it to be, but not so serious."

WHEN WE SEE A NEED

When we see a need
One in which we can surely heed
Will we sit silently by?
Will we hear our neighbor's cry?

When in the clutches of hopelessness
God does not resort to a panic
Mode of forgetfulness.
He gives us love and caring
From complete strangers who
Don't mind sharing.

With excuses we sometimes tell...
"We did not hear from God... well,
My friend. That will simply never sell."
For, God said in His word, "For as the body
without the spirit is dead, so faith without
works is dead also," (James 2:26).

We testify and justify
To sooth our conscious and sell our game.
But, nothing is ever changed
When we remain the same.

When riches are laid up for self-seeking gain,
When God said "GIVE" we felt such pain:
We dropped our heads and walked away,
"God, help us to know who made the day?"

We use our money (In God We Trust) –
To fight, kill and destroy, because it's about us.
Seldom do we question if we have enough.
Oh! The toys we create to us are worth.

Jesus said "For I was an hungred and ye gave me no
meat: I was thirsty, and ye gave me no drink: I was a

stranger, and ye took me not in: naked, and ye clothed me not: sick, and in prison, and ye visited me not." Then shall they also answer Him, saying, "Lord, when saw we thee an hungred, or athirst, or a stranger, or naked, or sick, or in prison, and did not minister unto thee?" Then shall He answer them, saying, "verily I say unto you, inasmuch as ye did it not to one of the least of these, ye did it not to me," (Matthew 25:42-45).

Reading III "Being Single"

"My soul, wait thou only upon God; for my expectation is from Him."

- Psalm 62:5

BEING SINGLE! THINKING SINGLE! ACTING SINGLE! BETTER KNOWN AS "FREE-FEMALES."

As defined by Merriam Webster, "a female ☺ is, @ "of, relating to or being the sex that bears young or produces eggs." (b) Pestillate. 2: Having some qualities (gentleness) associated with the female sex. 3. Designed with a hollow or grove into which a corresponding male part fits< - femelle Fr. M1 Femella, fr, L, girl, dim. Of femina la: female person: a woman or girl. B: an individual that bares young or produces large USA. Immobile gametes (as eggs) that are fertilized by small USA. Mobile gametes of a male. 2: a pestillate plant."

Sounds to me like "Merriam Webster" picked up on our mail, or do they know everything about us?

I have the female sex organs, but never used them to produce. I display some qualities of gentleness.

Pestillate is like having a pistol, but no bullets.

A hollow grove is like someone peering through my window, or what? Different languages have their spin on us. A woman or a girl-, I can agree. An individual that bears young or produce large immobile gametes (as eggs) that are fertilized by small mobile gametes of a male. I fully concur. It's like, I came, I saw, I did not conquer.

Not dismissing any above factualism in accordance with us being single... thinking single... acting single, we are Free-Females of which I see no dictionary documentation.

Being Free-Female; Telling yourself you dine alone each night because you might decide to bake a pie and not feel guilty by eating half of it at one setting because no one else wanted any.

Being Free-Female; Making a decision and buying a stupid expensive whatnot and convincing yourself you did it because no one objected.

Being Free-Female; Painting every room in the house a flaming red without having to listen to an echo.

Being Free-Female; Walking around your house all day in your birthday-suit and tempting no man.

Free-Female: Doing something really stupid and since there's no one around to affirm your stupidity you feel inclined to believe it wasn't so stupid after all.

Being Free-Female: Is having decided after being single forever... all her life, that one is better than 2. She keeps telling herself that after all, and the Lord God said "It is not good that man should be alone; I will make him an help meet for him," (Genesis 2:18). After all, He never said "it wasn't good for the woman to be alone."

The Free-Female; Believes she has mastered the single life... deserves all the accolades for doing so and states; emphatically, "everyone was not meant for marriage."

She believes she did it her way. A little temptation here or there was just an absurd illusion.

But, the nights she is restless and cannot sleep and she envisions her mate reading love poems to her. If she sleeps he will take her to dinner and order her the biggest lobster the gulf has to offer. Her next honeymoon will take place on the Orient. There's someone to cuddle up with when it's 1 degree outside and 2 degrees inside.

Be that as it may... a Free-Female imagine all those little ill-tempered kids at the park... the couple fighting next door about nothing, daddy's bad temper telling her that she is stupid... the husband that ran off with his neighbor's wife... the husband that turned out to be gay, anyway.

Honestly – is it better to want something you don't have or to have something you don't want ??????????????
???????? ????????????????????????????????????

Reading IV "Where Paradise Lives"

"When I consider thy Heavens, the work of thy fingers, the moon and the stars, which thou hast ordained;"

- Psalm 8:3

WHERE PARADISE LIVES

And the colors of leaves are not predicated upon seasons
of intensity...
waters were formed in a state of utter limpidness...
a single drip wash away all ruin.

Inflowing, always, never to be hindered or hindering,
time told of a place of forever: serene, doting...
my permit to enter, to see, to congregate, to inhabit
only for a little while.

And if you wanted a flower of a certain color
the want and wish was all that was needed.
Everything is set in a mode of piety, because you are
made pure.

Some had been there thousands of years, yet, their
garments still stood unstained. Not one dust of sin
ever crept in. I rested in a prevailing peacefulness
upon an atmosphere so appealing Van Gogh
would have breathed his last breath to capture.

Telepathy, Extrasensory Perception is the way of
communication. The internet would never catch up,
is deemed too slow. This explains why there is never
an unhealthy sound, only pleasantness and a healthy
indulgence of quietness.

A business prevailed, but what kind I knew not.
Time was not presented, just there: as if it always
had been and always will be. A whiteness prevailed,
not our whiteness, for we duplicated ours from
one that had already been authenticated.

One was unaware of self in an incensory sort of way.
You knew you were, but had no need; whatsoever,
to be attentive to self in any way.

It was as if I had always been there, always created,
never grew old: there was just the moment, there,
and the moment was always. It expanded itself with the
influx of souls and each soul was equally created.
I saw no one I knew personally, but I knew everyone and
everyone like me, I like everyone.

Each soul a part of the other, linkage, without any
part being separated, but each a whole... complete.
I asked, "where am I?" The answer! "This is Paradise."

THESE THINGS

A breath of peace flowed
from Father God to son Adam...
oozing through the fabric of human existence.

A covenant was engendered
upon the anonymity of human kind never
having to know the paleness
of war or its proclamation
of emptiness.

A peace so encompassing...
gravitating toward the
arms of love...
never needing to repent.
The two coupled with supreme happiness...
further down the
road joy awaited
bliss, together they met,
all joined hands and
on down they strolled to what
was forever meant to be.

Reading V "Adverse Conditions"

"He shall come down like rain upon the mown grass: as showers that water the earth."

- Psalm 72:6

ADVERSE CONDITIONS

There it goes again...
I can diffuse midnight breezes...
Along-side brilliant colored winds...

I take the blue breezes and hide them next to
My Spring garden of Daffodils and Magnolias.
The suppleness of sleep...
That walks over the coolness of night
May never see the full fruition
Of a lovely garden that grows
So well in spring

Adopting colors of pure holiness...
Only to fade under the blanket of
Dusty bowls...
They choose their garments well–
And flee from new seasons...
Only to grow up dead from blue breezes

BLACKBERRIES

I'm use to picking blackberries
in thickets so deep–
that dance around red hot sky on
sunny days bringing back memories
of juicy new fruit.
My tongue tickles with falling black sugar.
Fissures of popping ring up my ears.
My senses go wild!
Spices bubble!
Blazing syrup readies itself for a full
charade.
Blackberries pies are like that –
daunting toward a moment of peacefulness...
when hiding underneath a swelling moon.

ELIJAH! ELIJAH! WHERE DID YOUR RAVEN GO?

Elijah! Elijah! Where did your Raven go?
"Way far, someplace to
another assigned shore.
He never told me so.
This is another brand new day.
Where is breakfast? Maybe he lost his way.
I sure miss those fries and catfish.
That was really a tasty dish.
He was always right on schedule –
which is a pet peeve of mine.
Thanks for the cakes, stakes, tomatoes and potatoes.
Oh! What a continental breakfast last Sunday.
He always knew my fast day
and proceeded to go another way."

"God changed his assignment.
God changed my assignment.
I'm going down to Zarapath to
a widow woman's house:
Where, she will feed me there.
Maybe, we will meet again, brother Raven
Maybe, you will feed another prophet.
I hope you won't change your preacher menu –
my pallet is still salivating.
I can almost taste that fried chicken, now."

EAGLES DON'T FLY THEY SOAR!

A majestic feat in divine time
The magnificent birds show their ornate fine.
In a swirl of wind-full sky
The Eagle Eye keenly surge nigh
And condescend for others nearby.
Over above the uplift plain
Many never fear to cease their rein.

A fair play of show and tell
In a lissome way they did so well.
The wonder of nature haply apply...
In a place of prestige they sigh...
Beneath their clucks and clatter;
Yet, they glide as if it clearly matters.

Their ancestors roost mighty and strong
Only their offspring left alone
Carry the trait with flair
And split never forgotten winds
Where others have never been.
We tap our pens and write within.

BIRD AT MY WINDOW

It came out of somewhere,
that chirp, chirp was everywhere.

Not that I did at all mine –
to serenade me like this was ever so kind.

Although, I could not crack the code –
this chirp, chirp was certainly in the right mode.

God created it to be seen and heard –
if it could be understood it would not be a bird.

So, why are we having this little chatter?
Well, actually, it really doesn't matter.

Because, bird at my window came to rejoice,
I might as well sit back and just enjoy.

Chit, chit, chirp, chirp, choing, choing –
in a little while it will be going, going.

MISS BUTTERFLY

"Me and only me...
As like a flirting butterfly,
Fluttering myself from a hibernated cocoon
Into a glitz of gold,
I sweetened the month of May
Of blues, pinks, purple and radiance
And polluted hills bathed with beauty.
I kissed many flowers.
Love never suspends.
The morning dew never ends.
Sometimes captured and put in containers
Maybe to be stared and studied,
But only do I sing of spring and never
Seek revenge.
Under an uninhibited sky
No one ever question why
I go right along travelling more
Through variegated gardens to distant shores.
But, isn't this really what I'm all about?
It really is me and lonely me"

RELISH GOD'S VISIT TODAY

Relish God's visit today
when He rings your targeted door of heart –
open wide with arms to adore.
Let your spirit tingle and prance
that you were chosen for this blessed chance.
Oh! Hear Him tell –
you did well.

Reading VI "Take On Creation"

"His soul shall dwell at ease; and His seed shall inherit the earth."

- Psalm 25:13

A LITTLE TAKE ON CREATION

Way over yonder... if you
put your ear next to sand
you can hear the gluey rumbling
of planet earth as it was being formed.

God stood in the conduit of perpetuity
organizing one fleck of dirt... amassing
a link of souls about to become bodies.

From African Plains He accumulated Black Dirt.
From Mayan Foothills He gathered Brown Dirt.
From Swiss Alphas He reserved White Sand.
From Hindu Mines He collected Yellow Dust.
From American Knolls He assembled Red Clay,
and intermingled all specimens with His Love and
made man.

As Indian Chief (Rainwater) stood on the pinnacle
of America and tattooed poles of welcome; ships
traversed great waters to create a little rumble.

The African Tribesman hunted and gathered while
enjoying the wildlife of the open leafy terrain and
made crafts for cultures unborn.

The Magnificent Mayans turned out pots for drinking,
while, the Swiss figured out cheese holes to formulate
a better recipe. From Hindu Mines Buddha took charge
so as to perfect a religion.

I have yet to see a red hand attached to a black arm
attached to a yellow head with feet protruding
from a green leg. This would have been man's best
mistake.

WILTED WATER TILTED ENVIRONMENT

Drops of wilted rain
fell on tarns of unforgiving waters
filling up pools of stagnant squander
over years of forgetfulness.

Chief Grayhorse remembers the days
of clean fish jumping through glittering
green crispness... when his virgin tears
dripped lake friendliness.

Abiding near the untouched grip of
mans never ending grunge... an oppressive
mania of wooden forest... herbaceous borders
of long-ago, emptiness ravage the landscape
of chance.

I entered a time of blackness, where morose...
Social order journeyed the skies of human
precise; overtaking manner where fear would
dare go.

UNINHIBITED

Gawping at what I alleged to be an erroneous identity –
with grasping fingers and intense gaze –
this paltry piece of muddle,
I thought –
folded amid qualms of acumen –
was what?
Winded, dazed as if poised
between mania, a place of no splendor –
left no doubt in my mind, a place where
genuine stain up with genius, where harmony
was created there,
and, *there*, it was, *there*, it is, and *there*, it was meant to be.

LAZY DAYS BRING SUMMER

just sitting around on tired memories
grasping straws from last years' broom
of forgotten hopes... just sipping watered
tea lemons and honey dough cookies from
jars of stale cider...

just enjoying hot breezes of hazy thoughts
and unloading marshy grass as it tangles
traverse my forehead... just chewing words
and spitting them through long forgotten
alleys of erosion...

just watching knotty-tail Golden Retrievers
releasing themselves on unflattering fire
hydrants... just admiring the nimbly ant as
she methodically use whit consistently to
impact tables of starvation... just hanging
on every Song Bird's tale of tomorrows'
majestic whimper...

just being interrupted from just ... as it
machinate its' web of contorted thoughts of
uninvited whiffs of Fried Chicken and Collard
Greens stepping out of neighborly windows...

just reducing to bare bones, brainy makings
of nature, a green leaf without a hint of blue-
a brown tree without the privilege of crossing
over to become a man - a Stately Pompous
Pomeranian with gesticulations of blemish...

just seeking to absorb a hint of Miss Geranium's
newly cut Tulip Stems as aroma wisp athwart
my nostrils... just watching pure watermelons as
they liberate their growth and become expectant
with time...

just hypothesizing how a sister can stun the
male ego by putting one foot in front of the other
and stride down memory lane, jiggling...
last time I noticed, it was known as walking...

HEAR THE WHALES SINGING

Hullabaloo...
Certain times down by cool aged
Pacific, panorama overlay miles of
shoreline. Opportune times of year
big fish come calling... escalating...
from millions of years of histrionics,
an emergence so captivating...
necessitating man to surrender his stand.

Water suddenly disrupt-
thousands of pounds of nature
televise, "here
I am." They burst out after each
other, from here, there... reminiscent of
popping corn springing up from
hot melted butter.

Fashions of nature unleash
hidden talent across miles of
amazing joy. One's only expectation
encapsulate as much brain
waves as doable. The milieu for
this occurrence impale a stunning
precipitous miracle.

This show and chant continue.
An artist has no time
to finish his painting. A writer has
no time finish his book. I had no time
to untie notes, cords, melody, rhythm.
Give me a million years... that wasn't
enough time.

A DAY AT THE BEACH

Beaches in Southern California yield clues
of diverse history lying dormant through
eonaeons.

About 6'Oclock on a given morning
when sun give rise and mingle with surface
knick knacks... wind respire on pale blue.

As I locate my best moment,
along edges of sand and
sea water, little
ripples cascade between toes, shell fish, rocks and
tops of soda cans.

Looking out through space
imagining Dana's ship mask jumping from
the minds 'eye of time... makes one wonder.

A great lobster painted water a rosy pink, gingerly,
passing on its' way. A jogger's rock hound
trots, leaving three impressions and a gritty diamond
wedding ring.

A scant bikini top left by sunbathers told tales of tan,
impish behavior and youth at a premium. A picked
over chicken bone, banana peeling and sweet plastic
drink cartons gave way to hungry thoughts of days
gone by.

The sound of senior laughter, over-sized bodies
stuffed in sun and fun, left with no shame, went
journeying. Breakers opening to permit humans to
encroach, told of challenges yet to be exposed.

The waves play over the water... in a moment may
cease... leaving one to ponder... who was better for it?
The wind will go its' merry way... bumping its grace
all over again.

Time and again, thin blue water's welcoming mat
was always out with a sign saying "come, drown your
troubles, I will always keep your secrets."

Reading VII "Soul, Soul Salvation"

"Salvation belongeth unto the Lord: thy blessing is upon thy people."

- Psalm 3:8

SOUL, SOUL SALVATION

My soul was like a prowling wind.
Oh! How it whined away
like a clock of chimes anyway.
It ran, sat, it howled; bare, cold, alone,
fighting for some place to call home.

It searched to seize...
a little love it needed, but only
found emptiness like you wouldn't believe.
If I could only find the key...
this would not have to be.

Carefully I noticed when... oh, how it would
constantly pound within... that knock, knock
reminded me of a lonely harden rock.
"There must be a way," I say,
"to comfort this lonely heart, aye."

Finally, God finally heard my cry and
came so kindly.
How such agony had ended with peace –
within – without, though what a relief.
Thanks for my hearts Soul Salvation –
for sparing my life of total damnation.

MY SOUL SET SAIL ON A SHIP FOR AN UNKNOWN SEA

Far and wide
I ride the tide
As the awesome winds float my tresses where
And there;
No special place to be
While enjoyment creates for me.

As time has engaged itself unwell like a beaten bradawl –
And continents flee above the oceans of low –
I'm captivated by places I know not to be –
As the far-flung winds have lifted me to search and see.

A soul is the sum of a thing... Psyche-Essence-Effigy.
An educing the harvest of the best –
Hoping to attain a place of eternal rest...
And woe to those who miss the call
For in eternity there will be no more brawls.

There are graves yet to be dug and flatter me not
If I sigh not. Far-a-way distances still now I soar...
Lore of the things arrived at... places of uneasiness.
Continents gravitate to the next by way of sand and sea
Told by history of its adeptness of long-ago cease to be.

I reverence a spirit free to be innovative and liberating
No more enticed by scurry winds of lust and lout...
Vigorously exceeding places where mortals
Fantasize and romanticize of immortality...
Of a heaven of happiness that dare not cease to subsist.
A Holy Spirit will always rise above the gloomy tides
That once propagated its tumultuous bribes.

Woe! Death down to the bottom-less pit to ponder
Vigor from the holy of holies shall duly defy entry.
No flicker from above can penetrate or propel itself –
Only the sullied flames of hell must set solidly

Beneath the rainbows of colored seas and
Blench the oceans tides whose times of splendor
Will never hinder. The gallant and sleeping tattlers
Will never tell of the gold-lined pockets of those who
Are forever dead. Yellow Rose Petals whipping the wind
Of change... gaily shadowing swellings concealed between
Vile! That set sail on a ship of an unknown sea.

GOD NEVER FAILS

You might say "this just wasn't my day."
"Cheer up it's just a test anyway."
All your life time may not be rosy...
just lying in the arms of Jesus is quite cozy.

That vote that brought little hope,
just applaud. He will not let you fall.
Be assured God is still around and He
will not let you down.

Tomorrow, He will bring a Hallelujah
from on high; it will resonate and satisfy
the chambers of the heart with charity,
unconditionally.

Man is but a mission from God. His
assignment is as the passing of a
finger put to a hot stove-top.
Don't put your faith in him
for tomorrow is doubtful of his awakening.

God holds mysteries and truths that
He wants to convey to His individual
creation if we would only stop and
take time to listen. He is not a God of
ambiguity, but a God of clarity.

He is standing with open arms. His arms
only close when someone position inside
them; then, they close to give an embrace –
to console a depressed mind – to transform
a broken spirit – to soothe an aching heart.

So, press in close to God today and get your
daily dose of ecstasy not found in the world.

You do not have to look for Him – merely listen.
For, He stands before your every tacit word
just wanting and waiting to be heard.

LEARN TO USE GOD'S LIGHT

The light of a brand new day begins when we
awake. He spoke to the sun to run through the
darkness of another day. It is up to us to glory in
how He made the way.

His light saturating in your being penetrate through
the strife of life. No matter how dark your night –
God never diminishes His light.

If only you have small light shining through the bars
of your prison cell, this is a great story that you must
tell.

Over the course of a lifetime we cannot sum the
countless storms, rain and pain that comes to
destroy our gain.

With stretched canvas and the stroke of a brush great
painters harness the light to reveal a moment of
greatness we can only guess.

Light on a scope in the hands of a surgeon can structure
body parts untold. Light on the mind of God can
penetrate a heart and soul and make it whole.

It is always right to use God's light when it is bright.

HIS LOVE IS..!

His love is...
Not just when He spilled out
His life on the cross, but when
He refused to stay stretched out
grave ridden and paid the cost.

Not just when Jesus said to His
Father "I WILL GO." But the fact
that He was willing to go
uninvited, without any earthly
approval, no invitation from
kings or queen, without a *"what's
in it for me"* was sorpendente?

Not just when being born in a
lowly stable was unimportant,
but knowing that mankind could
be born again into the Kingdom of
God was important.

Not just enduring temptation and
rejecting it, but giving us the liberty
to do the same.

Not just suffering the scorn and scoff
of humankind, but giving us the grace
and resolve to quiet our tongues and
turn the other cheek.

GOD IS LIKE!

Two eyes of double love
that glares upon the horizon of a brand new day...

two legs of dual love that lends
leaping and running to the aid of men...

arms of equal love to clutch
personification of life's enthralling...

two lungs of look-a-like love,
furnishing air to living creatures as the...
breath of life...

nostrils of two-sided love,
enveloping morning's sweet breeze in the
midst of a honey rose...

two feet of equable love,
so as to rush to aid stray lost sheep...

ears that disburse attention
to God's many instructions and warnings
of life's spiritual awakenings...

doppelganger kidneys of love
that sweeps blood of its bad stuff...

ovaries and a fair amount of tubing
that keeps producing and producing and
producing produce...

small intestines apprise the large intestines,
"I may be small, but I'm astonishing."

A brain that says to the body,
"stick around you haven't seen half of my brilliance yet."

STANDING BELOW THE CROSS

Jesus stood tall on the Cross above.
I stood small on the ground below.

I could see His Glory shining
through His Blood Soaked Face.
He saw my story cloaked underneath
a yoke of sin.

His dialogue of communication was
of a Spiritual Nature; for, He never
uttered a single word, but
His joy of silence could soundly be heard.

I realized that Victory – Victory was what
the Cross was all about. As this
began to stream through my being... I stood
great and straight and almost broke a shout.

Clouds released a Heavenly Bounce.
Thunder took to rumble. Little surges of
wind blew as the day wore thin.

Jesus on the Cross engulfed in all
His Magnificent Brilliance commence to shine
through all His Godliness. I surmised
at that very moment that I was predestine to
win.

As His Blood slowly started to splatter – trickle
by trickle – I held out my trembling hands;
for this, in this milieu of time – I realized the
transpose gravity of a drop of His Holy Blood.

When His Cleansing Blood and my unclean
heart met each other a healing sensation
dawned. I realized then, the awesome power
that held one drop of His Living Blood.

BROKEN BODY (VS) A WHOLE SPIRIT

THE FLESH SAID,
"I cannot walk to my closet to get dressed.
I cannot get to my bath to get clean.
I cannot walk to my car to drive.
I cannot walk into the church once I arrive."

THE SPIRIT SAID,
"I can do all things through Christ who strengthens me."

THE FLESH SAID,
"I cannot reach my cabinets to get food.
I cannot get my chicken from the freezer.
I cannot light my oven.
I cannot walk around the kitchen to prepare my meals.
        Therefore, I cannot eat today."

THE SPIRIT SAID,
"I can do all things through Christ who strengthens me."

THE FLESH SAID,
"I went to dialysis today.
I have very little strength after my treatment.
I just feel lousy.
        Therefore, I cannot praise God today."

THE SPIRIT SAID,
"I can do all things through Christ who strengthens me."

The other day our sister in Christ exchanged her *Broken
Body* of immortality and put on a *New Body* of righteousness.
She ascended the staircase to Heaven with *New Legs*,
New feet and *New Kidneys*, and the spirit said to the flesh:
"*Guess what*?" "*I won*."

I ASKED

How big is God's Love?
He answered "Bigger than big."

How wide is God's Love?
He answered "Wider than wide."

How deep is God's Love?
He answered "Deeper than deep."

How long is God's Love?
He answered "Longer than long."

How high is God's Love?
He answered "Higher than high."

I know these to be true –
for one day He offered His big hand.

He spread His countenance wide.
He extended His touch deep.

He diminished His height low.
He reached His arms long –
and pulled me up from my pit of discontent.

DO YOUR VERY BEST

Do your very best
to pass the Godly test
the test starts now
and ends at death
no need to test alone
right now God sits Heavenly
on His throne
no trickery need be to take a guess
bound in the Bible the answers rest
search often to see
just where you need to be
because the heart will always tell
just how often you stumbled and fell
test of trials will come your way
so live your very best each and every day.

A LIGHT FROM HEAVEN

It was three days before Christmas,
as I lay a dying on my bathroom
floor in the middle of the night swollen
by darkness from door to door.

After reading the words of life all day
the letters seem to dance right off
the Biblical Pages that way.

As I listen to the quietness of the still
of night... I heard a voice that spoke.
"Everything my daughter will be
alright."

Pain was perfectly performing without
consent, but I knew by faith I did repent.
Suddenly, I glared up from a black space
through a colorless window into an Ebony Night.

A flicker... a pen of light cautiously penetrated
through layers of silent darkness.
The light entered through the top of my head
and streamed down my entire body
like you wouldn't believe.

As the light streamed through my body
the decaying disease of Lupus went out
of me and sin was cast asunder.

One day God stood on the clouds of Heaven
and flung the stars against a black sky.

That night He rode the <u>Heavenly Clouds</u>
once more and flung a flicker of light all
the way from Heaven into a sinful soul
and a decaying body and made it whole and
new again.

Reading VIII "Airports"

"Who satisfieth thy mouth with good things; so that thy youth is renewed like the eagle's."

- Psalm 103:5

AIRPORTS

While I'm sitting, expectantly, waiting to board
a plane... bags checked... ticket in hand... all that's
needed is the go ahead to board. "It often doesn't
happen that way... so quickly I mean."

So, you sit and wait... wait some more... scanning
gathering crowds, seeing more of what you may be
flying with, sitting with, eating with and talking with.

If I rattle around the nuisance long enough I may
come up with tales of little green and gray creatures
climbing elevators to top the skies of discoveries to
unknown or will be known destinations.

They scaled the walls of time sitting with the host of
the angelic and majestic. Imagine... pure water
falls, blue and sparkling... flowers never dying and
no waiting around elevators that light over the skies
like a thousand chandeliers that only twinkle to the
brides of their like creation.

A summons to board is called, but not for me, while
I'm still sitting, sitting and minding my own business.

I'm imagining a cloudless sky, my face pressed into
the window, a sip of 7up to tide up the next destination.

Intruding into my thought processes... seats are filling up
fast. The rude personalities erupt and I'm hoping my seat
is not next to a big mouth with a striped green, orange
and yellow something. "They can get loud you know."

If I decide to take off with the spacers on the next
available elevator and find out they left unhindered
miles ago before the arrival of the unprepared years
earlier... my feelings would be beyond devastating.

I can only envision the awe of an opportunity missed, of
splitting the unknown heavens... the exploration of fat eyed
creatures making foreign noises. Who knows what I will
be riding with, probably the one with the big mouth
and the green, yellow and orange something.

AFRICA

She stepped on God's earth one day
with diamonds waiting to be cut...
iron waiting to be melted...
lions sitting sprawled across
planes of sequins,

succulent tree meals waiting
to be plucked...
poets and writers waiting to be penned,

people so purple and sweet...
souls that run swift and deep
like cascading waters of Niagara.

Her beauty met up with
layers of pigment, canvas and hues...
capturing the eye of time.

Her wisdom... genius stemmed from great
queens and kings. Queen Nefertiti standing
powerful and beautiful... Queen Makeda, better
known as the (Queen of Sheba) traveled to Israel
to meet King Solomon. Menelik 2nd Emperior
of Ethiopia... defended his country against
Italian invaders. Shaka, a king of the Zulu and
a great fighter.

Her banks of history span long and wide.
Elephant's ivory tuffs... languages... mummies,
pyramids, wild life grace her landscapes as
enigmas known only to God.

Her mathematicians, scientists, farmers, craftsmen,
astronomers, doctors, towns, tools, kingdoms and
villages stood first and proud.

Africa!
Allow me to sit on your knee and run my fingers
through your leaves of lush?
Allow me to split your waves... scattering unblemished
love?
Allow me to dash my toes through your Ebony graveyard,
unmasking tidbits of untold genealogy?
Allow me to stand on Nubia and call out the pharaohs?

Allow me to sing the songs of your country
in a happy note?
Allow me to cook the tasty meals with the
recipes handed down by your ancestors?
Allow me to listen to the seniors and learn
the culture?
Allow me to gaze upon your Pyramids with
great wonder?

Allow me to ride your jungle and acquaint
the hump of the Camel and the eye of the
Elephant?
Allow me to dance in your desert and sip
the dust?
Allow me to laugh with the natives and
and swivel my red dress from afar?
Allow me to bounce the moon, twinkle under
the stars and chew the taste of your languages?

Thank you!

AVEC DIEU tout est. possible
(with God all things are possible)

TRAVELING AMERICA

Anytime, anywhere... I can be seen
streaking up and down the country.

Never did I boast of Luxury Dining or Lenox China
and powder rooms non-exist.
I glide through Talkative Concrete Cities, Aged Meadows,
Acid Towns and little known places hard to find.

My rates are reasonable and one luggage can take you far.
My hospitality extends from Monterrey to Marietta
as I offer you America...
Greyhound- Style.

In the chill of night face hard-pressed against squelchy glass
deep in the heart of Dixie
I counted stars until they lazily fell asleep
in corners of my bus window
and it was my time too.

Dreams of Oklahoma Chief's Chanting, Red Fish Drum beats
waking up bus passengers and rings of fog curling about creating
coronas seem to live again. Open fields that once festooned
centuries of Bison and Buffalo gave way to Rusty Plows,
Grubby Combines and Aged Chevy Trucks fixed in time.
Louisiana, Oklahoma, Alabama and Mississippi wastelands
depicted Fossilized Plantations that once rested on backs
of harsh labor. I all but envisioned burlap sacks
pounding hot hard earth lugged by seasoned calloused hands
stuck with sticky bulbs and hot blood striking pure white
cotton tainting its 'edges a washed out red.

After giving up a few bucks at a Nashville Diner
we cruised into the next city sluicing chicken grease
and hot soda between our teeth.

On Greyhound love interest was sparked
at St. Louis Coffee Stops and Chicago Gift Shops
that lingered from Detroit to D.C., igniting into full blown
flames only to be extinguished over a six-pack and condoms
latent on the beds of Motel 119.

CARMEL

Eyeballs arrive,
an affable sight, undue plunging waves
scattering the seashores of time;
downward, downward, liquid plummet, but
before meets with glaring glistening energy.

Heard of you, imagination glimmering;
a little smile aside, but not missing a stride,
over across the way peace abides.

Ever so inviting, only to taste your beauty –
beneath the midst of time; through the aptness
of nature you have become one of a kind.

Post cards scarcely convey –
a sweeping, dazzling array –
of what you're merrily seeing –
of what Genesis spoke into being.

Lingering memories –
in an enchanting day of mine –
simply leave me speechless and in a bind.
Oh Carmel! Help me to remind?

JUST AS I REMEMBER!!!

With jovial looks... anticipated ports-of-call...
luggage filled with requirements of formal attire...
awe inspiring bikinis... low cut swing
garments ready to test the sun and water in addition to glancing
male egos; we began to migrate under perfectly nurtured skies
and juicy blue waters begging to be sailed.

Our vessel yielded clues of stunning beauty... tested
travelers and gracious servants. Intermittent waves
welcome the luxury liner as if to say, "your sail is always
projected, your lakes are filled to capacity, your rivers run
deep, your oceans spread wide to accommodate your
lavishness."

With splendid dining, fish that once swam were now put at
rest under salt, pepper and precise formulas. Lobster gone cold
starred into mouths of over anticipated palates. Drinks of
suggestive nature later showed up as inebriated acts on ball-
room floors and staircases of intrusion.

Sounds of late night amusement penetrated the decks of
darkness and crackled the night. Little clothes-less Haitian Boys
leaped through ship waters... gulped freshly hurled coins from
ship passengers. Small earthy dirt floor shacks were
deemed as homes. Women walked for miles with head baskets
filled with family necessities. This was history book stuff
that stared squarely in ones 'face concerning something called
reality.

A petite Haitian school girl (Ann Marie) challenged us
to send books of learning to combat illiteracy and tackle
higher learning. A father stood brave and tall... only to
kneel to the grip of poverty each night before going to bed.

As the ship spread its luxury in sprawling fashion...
while wrapped up tourism was not a forgotten possession,
a little love letter was written across the hearts of many
and struck a cord as we departed difficulty almost to alien
to empathize.

SPRAWLING CITIES

Sprawling cities scatter their inhabitants
through a murk of morass.
They speak with intensity of moral sincerity;
laughs in public, but snivel out the inner nadir.
Oh! City of so many... city of so few...
your stance stays crouched from a wicked deal –
underneath a banner of in and out.
You were there last Sunday –
your leaning show for all to see.
They split through your paved and
naming of pompous streets where concrete
wed up with nostalgia.
Your many motifs enthuse – so many – so few.

OLD DUSTY ANTIQUE SHOP

Situated over across Charm Street
exist "Antiques Unique," upon entering
it's doors grandeur of past ages emerge.
Mildewed aroma jut around scented holdings
of hodgepodge. Corners of elite lives gone
by show on stained Victorian Couches.
Hallmarks of approval hover through
glass gilled shelves of whatnots.
Shoppers cuddle objects
of flaking paint, vanishing patterns and
termite threadbare wood
and are enamored.

Brimming crowds congregate in
Vociferous Tea Shops chatting over
addictive behavior and sipping hot brew from
Spode China. All Saturday afternoon hubbubs
wane as obscurity defy day, leaving dead
dreams and silly desires.

FAMILY RE-UNIONS ARE!

Meeting up after 20 years
with 400 pound relatives –
with buckle down pants, cruising in
laid-back Convertible Volkswagens.

Tables spread with can tuna,
fish tail sandwiches and
homemade fried onions.

That un-happy, un-employed, un-married
homeless 4.0 nerd still peevish about
why they unfairly foreclosed his 2 bath
mansion after 18 months of failed payments;
why he lost his job after 20 years of invalid
excuses for being late; why his ex kicked
him to the curb after 3 years and 4 nights
each week spent with the boys down at
Herman's pool and rib shack.

Little mischievous baggy-mouth boys
spiking Aunt Polly's 10 cups of red soda –
with dead toad legs and week old potato
salad rejected by the local down home flies.

Snuff-dipping and spitting
Uncle Benny with crusted-brown-dentures
still reminiscing about that 36-22-36, the
smart one that got away and the 40-40-40 one
he caught but wished she had gotten away
30 years ago.

Bubba the beer-gulping, Lysol-mouth
Would be comedian (of which every family
can boast of at least one) whose one liners
about why the chicken crossed the road went
South 200 years ago.

**FAMILY RE-UNIONS: THEY ONLY
COME WHEN YOU DECIDE TO GO.**

DID YOU MISS YOURS?

Reading IX "Life"

"Thou wilt show me the path of life: in thy presence is fullness of joy; at thy right hand there are pleasures for evermore."

- Psalm 16:11

LIFE!!!

"What is life?" I say...
"Just around that last corner...
just around the next breath...
toiling, tumbling, grasping, grabbing
         for..."

"Life, life, life! Come, come, come...
with all your handicaps, hang-ups,
indifferences, attitudes, leaping and
weeping; stop hiding in that corner."
I say.
         "Stop."

"Just yesterday you blossomed with
beautifulness; you were at your
height of loveliness... corners
were not a clue, suddenly,
         corners."

A SPIDERS'S WEB

Astonishingly, I stare,
as she journeyed through web layers.

With precise symmetrical lines it gyrated,
and sliced through gravity's relentless grip.
Ornaments of little black lines of perfection
split through centuries of instinct.

I just stood with child like perception and
could almost hear the next line as Charlotte
gracefully mesh corners of liberty.

LIFE GOES: LIFE GOES ON.
As thread slip through a needle eye
The flesh each day says goodbye
And where you're broken to pay the rent
You often wonder where it went
LIFE GOES: LIFE GOES ON

LIFE GOES: LIFE GOES ON
A few seasons somewhat bliss
Will to soon be sorely missed
By the early rising of each new moon
By the late rising of the body by noon
LIFE GOES: LIFE GOES ON

LIFE GOES: LIFE GOES ON
A standing mirror glass stately reminds
Of a lifetime to quickly absorbed by time
Leaving so soon a sticky matter
Leaving so late what a disaster
LIFE GOES: LIFE GOES ON

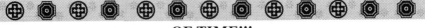

OF TIME!!!

No gaunt, nor glint, nor lout of time...
can ever erase the tone of chime...
standing below a pool of tipsy loom...
belted underneath a crispy gloom...
stepping into a lay of hefty doom...

as it goes and goes...
it adds to its statue a way that-
grows and grows...
once empowering a good youth,
now impassively lending itself to another
group...

with time in strain-
diminishing beneath swells of pain-
who could guess that time grows old,
unless a little whisper, no one would ever
be told...

Oh! Of time we so constantly meet.
Yea! Of time you gave me another feat
to greet another birthday, I applaud,
how you kept me in your space says just
about all.

In our time of youth our beauty stood
serene. Yet, we stick around just wanting
to rein supreme.

As we travel up the hill of will...
lets join minds and hands and simply
chill?

A new charm dress I bought with a strict
desire to pay the cost. Just trying to get
back the waste of pretty, we are no doubt
in this together.

Right around the waist time has not been
kind, but it seem to say "never mind, I'm
willing to stick around; you must learn to
be kind."

In night I lay dreaming in your sphere...
sometimes through a psyche of fear.

Sweet memories so numerous to recall...
often lends itself to joy that tells all.

a milk chocolate time dream –
one I never challenge to glean –
these I can hold dear,
whenever they thrust to come near.

Thank you for the sweet treats...
over yester years dawned so neat...
As you gave me space to wonder –
to glare upon a peace to ponder.

Just now I head up the road of time...
to contemplate triumphant this
quiescent life of mine.

Reading X "Death Of Teres"

"For this God is our God for ever and ever:
He will be our guide even unto death."

- Psalm 48:14

THE DEATH OF MY FRIEND TERES,
HER FRIEND ELVIS PRESLEY AND A
SAGA TOLD BY MRS. KAMAKAWA

Together they depart, serenely, befitting for one whose
being was embellished by fame
and the other whose self sought no egotistical limelight,
only for another. I

drew a deep sigh while cruising down a California
freeway as rain speckled by windshield, barely
remembering a Japanese Lady... Mrs. Kamakawa's
tale about rain and death.
It seems that, if rain occurs on the day of a death
or on the day a body is buried, that person's
soul enters Heaven – exclusively.

Elvis and Teres fixed in infinity, together, while I'm

spinning onto a tree lined street, where heavy showers
hasten, turning tree leaves sparkling... with thoughts as
weighty as deep water puddles forming around my car.

If a promise of something dropping from the sky endorse an
entrance to Heaven, "*I beg to die on a heavy rainy day.*" I
can always sip my sunshine once I've entered Pearly Gates.

Around her neck wind entwine stripes of pink, purple
and pale green, a Pure Silk Virgin Scarf. Smiles trickle
down her cherry cheeks as she present a birthday
card signed by the king. I could taste those days of

Chinese take out as we sat under Bitter Lemon Trees munching
sweet and sour outside the convalescent home and breaking
open fortune cookies... hoping for an excellent prophecy. Yes,

those skin wrinkle hands wiped down many tears,
like car windshield wipers scrubbing the rain. All
while, she draped a dazzling array of fish pearls, goblet
earrings and gold bracelets, drinking sun rays. It

was like that. I didn't mind her reminiscing as we
savor Big Reds and watch dew run down the bottles;
she relishing 22 years of employment her son gave Elvis
and her love toward the star as a mother to her child. I

shared her pain each time papers stained the celebrity
with a dreaded report. Now! To be no more! Deeming about
a feeble heart... gold ball point pens... Chinese empty take-out-
cartons, walks through the garden; letting go my love for
her and reawakening thoughts of him, as I envision their
eyes sinking deep behind August Dust somewhere near
Graceland and my yearning to say goodbye. Befitting.

WHAT ONE WONDERS!

On a deep murky night I irked a Jaded
sky on Mulholland Drive. A sign of purple thumped
beams of blue and scattered around my
yellow car whistling sonnets of gold.

Dashing beneath twigs of fallen stool stood
creatures of painful repute. A Holly-Bush
curled my messy main as air drenched my
tires.

Thoughts of loosing this crazed stalker
challenged my highest ideals. Cold clamored as
a chalice waiting to be announced.

Bellows of tiny creatures shadowed clatters of
quietness. Imagine, some gumption of my college
professor tonight. Everything hinged on Biology and
sex. He honestly proclaimed "Papa Hemingway
always rose to every challenge."

DR MARTIN LUTHER KING

His life was taken, but his hopes and dreams never to be forsaken.
The silence of his voice stands numerously tall in the ears of
    generations
who have yet to love or fear.

The distorted, windless body of an Emmitt Till, floating, dead, no
justice, no hope. The bodies of innocent, many swimming through
waters and draped by water hoses, living, some hope, life. Some
refuse to go down, stay down, and refuse to give up. All adding
necessary steps up the mountaintop struggle one climb at a time.

His demise was not in vain as he so eloquently stated, "a man who
    won't
die for something is not fit to live."

In the creation of things... some must die... some must live. Poets have
penned poems of death... dying. A beautiful Yellow Rose relent to
    death
after extending itself for a time of extraordinary beauty.

No assassin's bullet can wipe away everything. The hopes and
    dreams
of each can penetrate the depths of darkness and live through another
day.

His pen captivated the beliefs of his heart and soul as he so
    passionately
told. "When evil men plot, good men must plan. When evil men
    shout ugly
words of hatred, good men must commit themselves to the glories of
love. When evil men would seek to penetrate an unjust status, good men
must seek to bring a real order of justice."

"For we know in part, and we prophesy in part. But when that
    which is
perfect is come, then that which is in part shall be done away. For now

we see through a glass, darkly; but then face to face: now I know in
   part;
but then shall I know even as also I am known," (1 Corinthians
   13:9,10,12).

God! Please wash the dirt of destruction from our minds? Bleach our
hearts with the pure blood of Jesus? Take the pollution of pride
   from our
spirits? With your outstretched hands of mercy take the deadly
   grimy
germ of sin away and give us your all-encompassing Holy
   Medication of
everlasting life? Amen.

God gave us His perfect-prescription, Jesus Christ. Jesus death
   burial and
resurrection filled the prescription. Now we must take the prescription
and live.

COLUMBIA

On that Saturday morning
sun streaked through
a glisten cold
filled sky.

Suddenly, as I rest in bed,
tube working overtime,
there was this boom
on my house.

A broadcast announced, "Columbia
was 16 minutes overdue,"
16 minutes turned into
30 minutes, into 60 minutes...
60 minutes turned into 2 hours.

The Columbia Shuttle had tragically parted
over miles of cold crisp skies.

As the Columbia pieces spread far
and wide, a crew of
seven souls stepped out
on a Heavenly Cloud down
from below and climbed
into a higher behavior...
where they were warmly welcomed by a Heavenly God.

They boarded planes confident and without a doubt
knowing full well what they were all about.

Their driven hearts were filled with hate and every evil
intention was on their sick minds.

Their gunny sacks were filled with daggers... their choice
of weapons were waiting to be revealed to the flights
and crews later that day.

Death was their only aim; not just their own demise, but
the destruction of many, and this was no game.

As they neared their intended targets, driven by alacrity,
they were about to perform the unthinkable in a day and
way that will never be forgotten.

When steel met with steel and glass met with glass; the
chaos of such a deliberate, cruel, cataclysmic and
pernicious act against defenseless innocent life was met
with overwhelming pain, death and disbelief.

The entire planet earth watched that day... from East to
West, North to South and everywhere in between.

The world can only scantily wonder of the horror and
fear that gripped passengers and crews that day. Pain,
death, dying, many beautiful souls, they were all connected,
not just to each other, but to their creator.

Numerous might ask "Where was God that day?" For many
love ones who shed vases of tears... God wept for Lazarus...
He weeps for you. (John 11:32-35).

"The eyes of the Lord are in every place, beholding the evil and the good," (Proverbs 15:3).

For those who can't find comfort, Jesus said "I will not leave you comfortless; I will come to you," (John 14:18).

"Hereby know we that we dwell in Him, and He in us, because He hath given us of His Spirit," (1 John 4:13).

For those whose hearts are broken, Jesus said. "The spirit of the Lord is upon me, because He hath anointed me to preach the gospel to the poor; He hath sent me to heal the brokenhearted, to preach deliverance to the captives, and recovering of sight to the blind, to set at liberty them that are bruised,"(Luke 4:18).

"The spirit of the Lord God is upon me; because the Lord hath anointed me to preach good tidings unto the meek; He hath sent me to bind up the brokenhearted, to proclaim liberty to the captives, and the opening of the prison to them that are bound, To proclaim the acceptable year of the Lord, and the day of vengeance of our God; to comfort all that mourn; To appoint unto them that mourn in Zion, to give unto them beauty for ashes, the oil of joy for mourning, the garment of praise for the spirit of heaviness; that they may be called trees of righteousness, the planting of the Lord, that He might be glorified," (Isaiah 61:1-3).

"Humble yourselves therefore under the mighty hand of God, that He may exalt you in due time: Casting all your care upon Him; for He careth for you," (1 Peter 5:6,7).

Reading XI "The Indian's Chant"

"Lo, then would I wander far off, and remain in the wilderness."

- Psalm 55:7

THE INDIAN'S CHANT AND THE BUFFALO'S ROAM

I dawdle near a field in Oklahoma
Where lava rock burst out over the landscape akin to
Popping corn and summer wheat grass
Bathed itself in Miss Clairol's Fair-Haired-Blond
And tree-bark breathed a sigh of relief.
I could hear a hollow chant where Antediluvian Buffalo
Roam. I

permit myself to ooze centuries of
Incalculable loveliness... where
Indian wares were garlanded with natural
Shells from Cerulean Waters... where gods like
Crimson Nighthawk and Cute Shy Galaxy stopped
Off to bathe before returning to the universe of wonder.

Where blissful children submerge, croon and stay awhile
And swim with Fish Species approximating
Pink Gill Caruvan, Villamoni, Shamimon,
And dance through meadows dripping with loveliness.

"There goes that chant again!
That tells of the serenity of the soul –
And signal Gods to awaken –
That set Bison free
And gave Rembrandt's Lion its kingship –
Leveling playing fields between
Baroque, Impressionist, Renaissance and Classical."

As I watch midnight tiring...
To show my link of compassion to the God
I knew I should pick a star or two
And allow the moon to melt my mascara
And purify my piety
Before they fall sleepy in corners of my car windows
Creating little crater dimples on my windshield.

WHERE THE FOREST LIVES

"This is a very pretty place...
Where squirrels build houses from old nuts –
Where hanging tree moss crystallize into
Pink Ice Sickles,
Where the skins of buffalo wear their
Wrinkles very well –
Where snakes go on diets to loose the fat
Around their hips. This is a lovely place
Where basketball player's shoes are measured
From the imprint of dinosaur feet –
Where a single dead leaf can blow itself
A hundred miles and yet feel right at home.
A Turtle Hump often means shelter from the bomb,
Where frogs sing night songs to awaken the
Sleeping forest.
Where the rabbit hops genteel right into her next season,
Where the trees swing and sway with the storm,
Yet still stand tall.
Such a charming place,
Where the streams run and run and never hide,
Where the butterfly wear its dress from a
Designer pattern.
Such a fetching place.
Where the bear borrows honey and never repay,
And the silliness of trapping mummies that went
To capture their gold.
Just so adorable... just so neat.
The little nimbly ant told holy secrets its 'grandmother
Fear to go.
Oh! So untidy... the cupidity of the other creation
To gun on the dear that mimics the right of nature.
We long to play cricket with the swelling of the noise."

SPREADING POSSIBILITIES

I picked Autumn that dared not to blossom.
Its pink and purple weighted light
under the heaviness of Winter's possibilities
past.

Harshness so corrupted the spread
of everything so-nice, so-deep, so-pure.
In times of stagnant one must wait
for the slow seducing of natures enticement.

After a period of subdue, the glassy eyed glamour
of an unsullied generation unwrap its
diffidence - disseminating like whose who -
on a parity of freshly hewn splendor.

When midnight dares to arrive so soon –
and puts on its innocence before day –
affability get hitched to timing of nature –
and distribute its purity.

Reading XII "Stopover With Masters"

"Thou hast ascended on high, thou hast led captivity captive; thou hast received gifts for men; yea, for the rebellious also, that the Lord God might dwell among them."

- Psalm 68:18

A STOPOVER WITH THE MASTERS

Canvas rolled down, paint
embraced silhouette of safe-haven.
Mohair from brush tipped
Dali's (Sacrament of The Last Supper)
as Monet's radical strokes pivot
highlights of nimble water with drifting sleepy
sailboats.

Sandro bathed (Venus) in soft golden light.
Centuries ago, Leonardo over in Vinci
was caught putting his last vestige on the saints
of old.

Whereabouts of Michelangelo could be detected protruding
over the (Sistine Chapel Ceiling) as God amalgamate
with prophet Moses.

Within distance I could see
Gainsborough's rapidity blessing us all the
way from Sudbury, Suffolk with cool
fresh greens, blues, as if delimited
by pools and skies scuffling to emerge on a crispy
day.

Cezanne's four impressionist peaches
grew more succulent as one fell softly from
a table onto my feet, splitting pigments of
yellow and burnt orange.

The impressionist left me with an impression to
daub a speck of yellow and finish the last attainment.

A GRAND DEBUT

Yes. Michelangelo undraped her, like David,
dusting sands of marble, proudly
stepping forth from 6 generations. A grand
debut from teeth to toe; her beauty did not
omit a tempo. Her long head peace seem to
float in space as if provoked by great puffs of air.
Donatello, Giovanni, Ghirlandaio, Bubens,
Raphael saw her; as she majestically poised
her nakedness with a cloistered hand. Now
Michelangelo, you charted the human figure
for umpteens yet unborn, chiseling
your way to unmatched genius-
inspiring onlookers as they forgot
imperfections of their own physique.
Your hunks of white marble dotted terrains
like herds of pale elephants peripatetic
from Caprice to Florence. You passed on your
quill to finish a poem-your scalpel to chisel a
form-your architectural schematics to finish
a house-your paint brushes and oils to finish that
painting, someday.

THE WONDERMENT OF NATURE

The galaxy glow light waving beams...
Above an earth that summons its sheen.
In a dashing prevailing atmosphere
Lay a sustaining glee gyro frequency hemisphere.

The star light twinkles brightly.
The morning glory tiptoes lightly.
As God showed Abraham stars of his family,
It was a covenant never to be gambled.
With His promises He never withholds.
They have already been written
For generations to be told.

Sitting above the sky... what a name...
One in which angels reverence to proclaim.

Stargazers, astronomer "Benjamin Banneker"
Lived to tell how his telescope served so well.
Astronauts search to see
What God already planned to be,
Stars will keep condescending
Their scintillation forever...
As we gaze into Heaven from our back doors.

In thee lies the wit of wit
In which no human is capable
Of bargaining with.

Henceforth! The wonderment of nature's
Smile draws nigh...
As galaxies so sweetly go traveling by.
Stars have stood the test of time;
Unmatched,
As they recline in the lap of nature and
Claim just that.

Reading XIII "Though I Dare"

"The seed also of His servants shall inherit it: and they that love His' name shall dwell therein."

- Psalm 69:36

THOUGH I DARE TO SAY

I.

Though I dare to say... of an embodiment of time with the tell of feelings of an affection named thus so.

II.

A time, a feeling of strength of mind to name that which is... that which has come to be... that which if filled with warmth glowing in a heart that never thought would be.

III.

Oh! Some have told of stories so fine that match the harmony of the love in their hearts... of dreams to be seen, but gradually, finally, splattered upon the horizon in a day, a time, a place not so planned.

IV.

We know in ways others will never, or will ever need to know. Each to his or her own experiences to behold the despondency or the serendipity of details.

V.

It is of no great secret of love shared by those who have not entitled themselves through no enforcement of mind nor heart to share what perhaps God Himself have meant to be. Only the lonely dare deny, they should never deny. It's not for them to know, assuredly.

VI.

The evolved involved can only tell of the most dear of thoughts held so softly in hearts submerged simply by hope. A hope incorporating itself... to break through... to burst forth with tentacles reaching wide to embody the other's tentacles that spread so far.

VII.

We, you and I will dance through the love field of joy picking the ripeness of plum felt endeavors of what happen so sweetly meant to be. The integrated are not required to tell, only to reverence the glow of spiritual and emotional cords intertwined by nature.

CAUSES

For all the causes to wonder
I intensely create pillows of light clouds.
Thoughts sometimes engendering pale pink things,
horizons not yet conjured.
Over by countless cravings of green thunder
I often wisely envision
mystical life filled with indebted goodbyes.
What with all the hysteria,
doubts, sagacious times gone by,
curious pinning for gaudily gain
makes one speculate about wishes of callous authenticity.
Beyond over-bearing views stand particulars.
Justified passion bind to the fringes of the basis of era
creating newly mesmeric smatterings of long held imaginings.

ME, ME, AND ME

Swashbuckling through the youth of time
made each step seem like a glass so fine.

As the eye of gleam stare clear of glasses,
err, all my ways were loud and sassy.
My time to laugh came mild and sweet;
Like dawn of freshly aroma rolling over my feet.
Oh! Err, Heaven you created a brand like me.

Undulating over from styles of new...
accelerating full speed trying to catch up with
yesterdays morning dew and binding
up two bellies for new suits for selling–
shaking off fat like bowls of jelly–
oh! Err, Heaven, what is happening to me, me?

As grey hair showed, millimeter by silly liter–
from a sister who never ruminated of escalating
toward old. Tender softness of bare immunity had
ever so penetrated through stains of creepy sights;
such like, freshly brewed wrinkles – creaky joints –
bothersome pain, told of too much labor, of labor
in vain. Dimness shadow the door of disbelief
that stared upon my Heavenly Seat, where globs
of unused goop leaned toward a mantle of a
hopeful new year. Oh! Err, whatever happened
to me, me, me?

As time has fragmented my wound of guess-
I don't have time to take care of this mess.
As you can see I'm doing my best, please
stop singling me out from all rest?
Oh! Err.

ME AND THE LADY

Streaming through a tempest night
stood a fading golden candle
filled with melted memories of
flickered hopes gone by.

Glasses of almost empty gleam,
bowels of half cold salads,
less danced blues notes
loosing their swing, lingered,
as she drowned her expectations
of a love never to be.

Years rolled... he never showed.
The lady would often cry,
as I shimmered quietly by.

To grace this lady
was more a privilege,
never a chore.
I ignited her glow.
I glint her hopes;
through years of silent togetherness...
just me and the lady.

IMPORTANCE

The would be necessities for constituting a
heart like hers was indisputable.
Bubbly beneath silver wings lie a
thrashing mechanism of chase gold.
While, oxygen and warm AB positive cascade like
streams of confetti on green trees during
a cozy Christmas wingding.
Where, deepest faith and fervor interweave like
alternating square knots intervening love knots.
Translucency fashioned her,
enticing sugariness of her spirit mesmerizing
morsels of Eastern Sunshine.
She is annulled of any hint of scandal.

They were overjoyed to meet after a long season of sorrow
and presupposed a fresh beginning.
She left only her memory to transpose
corridors of time.
Articulacy of her smile, ways in which she
cosset her identity can be akin to delicate rain falling
to infant flower petals cuddling sonnets of tranquil
infatuation.

I SO OFTEN

I so often taunt my imagination of epochs gone by.
If and only I could bring back the days of youth,
hellos and goodbyes would be filled with
merriment, pleasant aroma of commonness
saturating bones from ending to ending,
almost not containing the melodies of hallowed
reminiscences.

I so often evoke that which
should not have happen, waiting days to do
something, but did nothing... nothing that I
sought to do was important. The will to do was
washed out by the necessity of what was to be
pragmatic.

I so often regressed, then overwhelmingly
imparted my liberty to the sincerity of nature.
But, daunting responsibilities erased the necessity
for acceptable malleability.

We may have seen, we hay have known, we may
have done, we may have gone, we may have been
...in the final... what will we be?

REFLECTIONS!!!

We're given time and space to fill...
A distance between birth and death...
An occupation embarked... what a thrill
To know a thing and do it best.
The misty night before dawn creeps.
An uncertain prowler refused to sleep.
Wind sours through the chimes of brome.
Reflections run deep.
A solitary mood is near.
After all is done... small time to weep;
Simply, hold to that which is dear.
The awe of miracles!
The fire by night... the cloud by day, (Exodus 13:22).
The hand touching the hem of His garment,
(Matthew 9:21).
The dust that became man, (Genesis 2:7).
The empty tomb... Sara's barren womb, (Luke 24:6),
(Genesis 18:10).
It's time for THANKSGIVING...
For the Genesis of God's Revelation.

NEVER REMEMBER TO TRY AND FORGET

Her teeth sheen like virgin raisins on pitted sunbeams.
That walk was quite the stuff not made of proper innocence.
She captured old Tom Wey by way of a Dilapidated Soldier's
Letter that showed up in the, "Advertising Wife Newspaper
Column."

Old Tom Wey left the war and hoped a train for Siege Moore
Plains. It was an awfully hot and dry day, but old Tom Wey
was destine to luck in on this bright and sunny fairy-tale.

Most around Siege Moore Plains would say old Tom showed
his hand awfully early, but newspapers get old after one
day. Tom surmised after many years he'd left most of his
smarts somewhere before he boarded the train for Siege Moore
Plains.

He could only assemble greasy whiffs from the stains of her
Hot water cornbread as he occupied the warm spot where she often
reclined. Her stockings still danced down the bathroom door and
the thought of her perfume peeved his nostrils like a scented boar.

Only if old Tom could sum up what went wrong. Was it too
much hunting without capturing any game? Perhaps, it was the
fishing gear he spent more hours with than she, or the times he
forgot to leave words of appreciation for her sassy walk; times
he didn't properly thank her for making an old soldier content
just by cuddling him through nights of thunderous rain.

She picked up and left well-nigh two years ago and old Tom
and his new bride never tire of smothered liver and onions
and potato pie. The blushing bride only made hot-water-cornbread
during nights of thunderous rains.

A TINGE OF GOLD

Fields surrounding Vietnam
whimper like the sadness of a widow
after turbulence of a storm.

A tiny Vietnamese Lady wrapped up
her green eyed American Boy.
She dreamed of pasty foreign hands caressing
her yellow face as they once did during times
of uncertainty.

As rumors of war deceased long ago,
so did her hopes of a SOLID HOME, CROWDED
CITIES and DESKS of WRITING.

He went home to a DODGE, a MISS CLAIROL BRIDE,
a STREAKED GRAY CAT, two LAZY DOGS, a
TEENAGE PIZZA LOVING SON and a DAUGHTER
with BLUE HAIR and LOUD MUSIC, an EIGHT to
SIX and ALL THE TRAFFIC HE COULD CLING TO.

That green eyed boy married, lived with
his somewhat two American gray and brown eyed boys,
his charcoal hair wife amidst fields of foreign
skirmish and hostile memories.

That tiny lady looped her long gray braids like
that streaked gray cat curling his tail around
recollections of his long departed grandparents.

She remembered how the moon dangled a special significance
over her cloudy chartreuse, as she danced
graves where grass would not grow and canonized
her American Green Eyed Boy.

Reading XIV "McDade Tapestry"

"For thou art great, and doest wondrous things: thou art God alone."

- Psalm 86:10

Woven through the tapestry of "McDade-Grand-Women"
flow attention grabbing threads of varied colors.

There are those who symbolize the vigorous green thread
of life...
"The Chlorophyll Women."
They have their hands on the green light of go.
They must grow... they must do... they must see and they
must conquer.

Some whose threads run pink display a continuous
flow of energy and excitement. They are joyful, witty
and create storehouses of laughter and amusement...
they are known as...
"The Merry Women."

Characterized by red threads and the hot blood of
diversity and temperament stands...
"The Red Rooster Women,"
always eager to climb into the ring with any opponent for
another match... often without checking their equipment
for wear and tear.

There are the yellow threads...
"The Caution Light Women."
Vigilant, yet optimistic... before taking the next step, they
always test waters for shark debris before stepping into
the "bubble-bath of life."

The brown threads can seem separated, feel isolated, discreet,
independent and often do their own thing...
"The Sugary Brown Beauties."

Threaded Royal Blue and debonair...
composing a "Stella-Performance" ...but neither Broadway
nor Hollywood is interested... personify

"The Blue Goose Women." They have mammoth ideas, boast
of little or no green to finance the reality of their dreams.

Stitched white threads of "Biblical Truth" classify
"The Set Free Women."
They stitch threads of purity not overburdened with criticism
or cornucopia. They try to keep the tapestry clean and on
course without spot or wrinkle.

Orange threads can subsist in true doubt...
"The Pullet Women."
Alas, speckles of heavy duty force counteract
their best intentions. Many times when the Red
Rooster swagger the Pullet takes note.

In total they bring to the tapestry a commonsensical work
of art. Their individual threads are frequently mixing...
sporadically crisscrossing, yet still growing separately...
guardedly optimistic and caring and so it is. The
Magnificent "McDade-Grand-Tapestry" moves on.

WOMAN

She starts life keenly attuned...
straight from her mother's womb.
The responsibilities she must adhere...
lies just beneath her surface near.

Her surface speedily wears bare...
exposed to the world as an open stare.
It is always a blessing to view her charm,
love, goodness, not just a con.

Life dares her to a huge challenge;
yet though, one she always seem to balance.
She supersedes life's many roles
without even a hint of growing old.

The many acts on the stage of life she performs
can definitely not be considered the norm.
Consequences only make her better like vintage
wine... one can tell by her strut that she is perfected
by time.

Her glory is Heavenly Bound,
all that whisper about her, O! Just listen to the
sound. Her adjudicators can only glare, because
there's something in her physical resume that says
"you don't dare."

One may say "there's a secret to all this."
"I guarantee it's one I sadly missed."
But, she always knew, because she started life keenly
attuned straight from her mother's womb.

HOW DO YOU KNOW WHEN YOU ARE OLD?

If your next birthday is just around the corner and you have gotten comfortable with the 11 months and 29 days of your previous birthday and hesitate to write the next number,

OR,

When mother-nature completely relent to father-time without any attempt of a compromise,

OR,

When you sit at the kitchen table to eat your bowl of cereal and discover that it's still in the cereal box on the stove,

OR,

When you tell your friends your age and the only word they can find to say is "WOW."

OR,

When you are looking in the mirror applying wrinkle cream and have to reach for the second jar,

OR,

When the same tube of makeup use to last 30 days but now only last 21 days and you think the tube is getting shorter,

OR,

When you have more lip stick above and below your lips than you have on your lips and you wonder why the tube emptied so soon, or why your co-workers think it is time for you to retire,

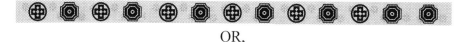

OR,

When your wrinkles support the glasses on your face without any support from your nose,

OR,

When you stare at your face in the mirror and try to figure out the best Side,

OR,

When you water your artificial plants and your real plants die and you wonder why,

OR,

When they stop sending you discount advertisement coupons for sheer panty hose, four inch heels and exercise equipment and start sending you coupons for support stockings, orthopedic shoes, scooters,
walkers and wheelchairs,

OR,

When none of the above applies to the mind that thinks or fails to think,

OR,

WHEN YOUR BIRTHDAY IS THANKSGIVING

When your birthday is Thanksgiving
it is really so neat.
I thank God He chose to give me and
others this blessed treat.
Just knowing it is simply not another day...
is a fantastic miracle in every way.
Early at 5AM I entered God's earth.
But, this was His chosen time for my birth.
The aroma of turkey many new mothers could smell.
Many years later they would often tell.
Sometimes I felt guilty for spoiling my mother's holiday.
But, I never heard her say.
Thanksgiving is a special time for praise...
God's blessings are great for many days.
When the year is almost gone...
we must give thanks that many things did not go wrong.
Thanksgiving should be a time of rest;
after we give God our very best.
Paint your day a lovely life.
Trust God to take away all strife.
This special time is simply not tradition...
it is a God given mission.
Our father has given us a test of time;
one in which we can have great peace of mind.

Reading XV "Inauguration Day"

"Hearken unto the voice of my cry, my king, and my God: for unto thee will I pray."

- Psalm 5:2

INAUGURATION DAY AND CELEBRATION

They linger by the millions, placated by the anticipation
Soon to be act of transformation.
As we – they and the entire world observe history
In the making. Oh! And afterwards – not just any history;
Not just olden time history – not just the past history
Repeating itself again and again stuff...

But a chronicle – with connected joy-reverberating through
Standstill ancestral chocolate souls. Oh! They too hear...
They too know that their sacrifice did not reach a vain point...

They regret nothing to the max... yet conjoined... coincided
With tranquil rumpus of past proceedings on planet earth.
A place from weariness to rest is being made into material
Of historical perplexity...

When I'm about to drown in my own tears... the black joy
Tears of my ancestors swing from the rafters of paradise.
The gleeful sound of such weeping – such rejoicing – such
Attainment – "I can only glow..."

"Momma, Dr. King, Sister Coretta, Momma Bethune,
Mother Rosa Parks... I didn't know you Ladies
Could swing like that. It's a Holy Swing from on High.
Oh! Don't be bashful girls, nothing to be bashful about –
Barack won't mind, nah, not one bit. A party is going on.
We are celebrating. I see y'all got healed from Arthur and
All his riders, must be nice... not a stiff bone in the Joint...

Oh! I see Africa over yonder... where the Obama relatives
And neighbors are tapping to the beat of old bucolic drums.
And the dust of their ancestors are blowing through the
Wind. Wow! This thing is catching on Big – like wildfire...

Hawaii is coming in. Oolala! The grass skirts are shaking in Change...

Europe, Asia and all down under Australia, people all over the Planets are getting the groove. I hear Africa and Antarctica Chilling out... way-to-go! Got-to-Love-it! God Bless!"

WRITTEN ON INAUGURATION DAY – JANUARY 20, 2009

Reading XVI "A Terrorist"

"Thou through thy commandments hast made me wiser than mine enemies: for they are ever with me."

- Psalm 119:98

THERE'S A TERRORIST AT THE GAS TANK

He sets there, regular, supreme and super-supreme,
day after day.
You pass his situation and look over anyway.
You know you must adhere. When he beckons
you come near,
cause your gas hand sets on next to none.
Finally, you relent to his uncompromising call.
After you fill up and leave he has taken all.

                            Cause he's legal

His prices keep climbing every time you shop.
You know you're being high-jacked each time
you make that stop.

                            Cause he's legal

You must take money from other necessities,
food, clothing, shelter, health-care, but he is
driven by obsession and greed and not your need.

                            Cause he's legal

He stands with no law book, Bible or gun, but he
is altogether legal.
Some drivers have lethal weapons in their cars,
but it's illegal to draw down on a gas tank.

                            Cause he's legal

He stands stately tall and he knows you will be back
soon and his prices will have risen by noon.

                            Cause he's legal

"Empty your wallet," the terrorist says, "next time
bring more money."

We sit, wonder, watch and pray that the terrorist will
some day soon, "have mercy on us," we say. At
home we dialog around the kitchen computer table

how some are paying. After all, "we can do without the take out cappuccino, trade in the SUV for a Toyota something. It really is quite extravagant to patronize Mcrobbs, Carol-Outside-the-Box and Libby's Establishments."

Cause the Terrorist is legal

IF YOU FIND A TERRORIST UNDER YOUR BED!

You will not be able to call
"Homeland Security" –
you would never get through...
you would be tagged a "Psycophobia Idiot"
when they come for you
with straight-jacket.
You will be hurried to a ward known as crazy.
You will be gone...
and the terrorist will still be under your bed.

"Instead! When you find a terrorist under you bed...
be inquisitive! Be very inquisitive!"

"You see... he needs to be captured!
He needs to be captured – now!!!

Listen... always keep a netted rope
inside your big bedside stand...
for when he comes out, net him... yes, rope him,
don't hang him!

Tie him to the bed... for you do not want him to
escape...
that would prove a mistake... a mistake indeed!!!!

Find a comfortable chair... no, not for the terrorist,
for you.

Sit and get comfortable.
After you have reached your comfort zone...
stare him dead in the eye... smile and keep smiling;
for the spoken word might not be understood.

Meanwhile, take the time
to notice if he has two eyes, two ears, two hands, two

legs with feet attached,
a mouth and nose.

If all the above are so...
ask yourself, could he be in any way human,
like me?
Could he be prone to sins and mistakes, like me?"

Look deep into his eyes...
Deep... Deep...
as deep as the rain that falls from Heaven and
sprinkles the grass below.

Deep... as deep as you search your pants pockets
to find tax money for the 'IRS,'
as deep as you search the trash can outside the
lottery store.

Let the created energy of your deep delicate Spirit
flow deep into his terrorist soul.

Listen deep for the answer to the prayer you prayed
as you knelt before God on...

YESTERDAY!

"If you save my soul Lord,
I will love my neighbor.

If you save my soul Lord,
I will love and pray for my enemy.

If you save my soul Lord,
I will work in your kingdom and be fishers of men.

Lord. Send me someone to witness to?"
If you are sure and only if
you are very, very sure you heard the
Spirit of God speaking,

run! Run!
Run for your Spiritual Sword (Bible).

If the terrorist speaks to you in plain speech and say,
"Ma'am, sir... I am no terrorist. I am a thief.
I came to steal whatever is of value, but you have
shown me something more valuable than money.
You have shown me the greatest treasure your
home could hold.

You have shown me love.
You have shown me compassion.
You have shown me faith.
You have shown me God."

Jesus sat in a boat in Lake Gen-nes-a-ret
and told the disciples to let
down their nets for a draught
(Luke 5).

The disciples obeyed and let down their nets
and brought up an overflow of fish.

Jesus said. "I will make you fishers of men."

"The netted rope did come in good. Bravo!
You have become a fisher of men and
I have told a great fish story.

But if your deep spirit did not hear
from Jesus' Spirit...

you and the terrorist are on your own... because

I'm all out of ideas..."

THE FEET TREAD THE CRIES OF THE
UNREST AS THE VALLEY HOLLOWS

The steps of wingtips on newly shined hard-wood floors
In Wash-chin-ton reverberates like cadences
Of I-rack bomb shells.

But pa-toons in Mo-zeal have learned to decipher the
Wash-in-ton wingtip cadences.

Ten O'clock wingtips marching to swank con-dress-inol
Hide-ways command troops to listen. Wait!!! Hear the
Beats, stepping, clink, clink, bang.
Ears to sky-ways, listen, I'm reading the wings as
They tip the halls, problem solved, states won't
Be getting to war stuff today... other pressing matters
On agenda, like scen-ate pay-raise, early golf-game to-day.

Little boy and girl in Bang-la-dish sits on garbage dump.
But, wait, they to have heard the cadences, learned at
Three to decipher the code, their little bloated
Growling bellies cry out no, food or aid today, back to the old
Search-dump way.

A slick black banana mostly skin, a step up from
Yesterday... rotting sardines!

They hear their mommy talk about a far away
Land... "A-merry-re-ca" ...she states. "They eat too much
Stake – cows and big red over grown craw-fish,
Called lob-lob-lob-stirs."

"I hear the press-i-dents pay for them. Somebody
Name George Wash-chin-ton." Mommy said, "they
Take little pictures of them and put them on green paper."
She said, "they look old... like they lived a
Long time ago."

"I hear them A-merry-re-cans fight over them old green men,
And, go and steal some old big ones named Franklin, Grant,
Jefferson and Lincoln right out of their resting places."

"Too many can get heavy, but I don't know how." She said.
"After a hundred years seem like they no more than
Green bones. Bones don't weigh much, unless you get an
Awful lot of them."

"I hear they don't talk... they don't move an eye-ball, but
They got power."

"They put writing from a book on the back of them little
Dead green men. I think they say do no steal, no something
About trusting in a person named God. I guess if you have
Enough of those green men you don't need to read no
Book."

Little ones in Sue-dan hear the cadences, they cry out from
Overt hunger, the tips of the wings predict many more
Days –
Days of No, No, No, No food
Days of No, No, No, No time to care today
Days of No, No, No, No I'm busy
Shivers, times of tribulation
Ages of trepidation
Stages of loiter, turned pages to soiled discontent
Heard all the way to Blue-Ridge-country.

Where little bellies remember the cadence from home
Songs from Wash-chin-ton of long ago
They didn't cry... they dared to die
Just dilapidated around cold cut whispers of starvation.

Many over the world cry out to sorrow –
Where others never had any intent to borrow –
But reign will tell –
Of just who forfeited so much to allocate so little!

FUMING TWISTER

In the middle of the day-
wind began to pick up and
a few drops of rain fell here and there.
The sun stepped back; while,
dark clouds moved forward.
The sky became illuminated with volts of electricity.
Mom shouted. "Children, come into the house."
Doors closed, windows shut.
The head count included mom and five siblings.
Mother prayed and walked the floor.
The rain pounded; the lightening sparkled; the
thunder roared and the wind howled.
Some siblings hid under the bed; but, I began to
seriously wonder about our survival.
If we would have another chance-
to beat up on each other again-
to race each other home from school-
to get that first slice of warm soggy ginger bread-
to wear our three dollar sneakers long enough-
to see our toes stick out through the top-
to sit on the porch and see who could spit
grape seeds the farthest, was at issue.
My thoughts were suddenly interrupted by calm
breaking in from everywhere.
Six souls stepped outside; whereas,
our little bleached house
was removed from it's foundation-
it remained intact; and, people from all
corners of that little Louisiana town
came to witness what newspapers referred to
as a modern day Noah's Ark.

THE UNTOUCHED TREASURE

He entered the middle of the night...
not by candle light, but by pure might.

Oh! How he sashayed with dominion through
room after room as a Cyclonic Sirocco sweeping over
Malta.

No thought was given to carefulness or neatness...
for this was a thief – you see.

The sound of bargain costume jewelry conjugating with
wood and glass could be heard as he scoured and toiled
for sights of flashing Tiffany and the appearance of a
flash of silver something.

No splendor or large spending bills appeared.
A dime or two could be heaped, but no big discoveries.

Thievery whispered in the ear of the thief that he should
escape as he whisked pass rooms laden with garage
fake-not's and flee market what-not's.

Sadness gloomed over spirits of the household.
Dropped expectations of the greatest riches were never tapped.

You see... on the Coffee Table rest a map (Holy Bible).
A masterpiece of clues to the greatest treasures conceivable...
was never tapped, but passed up.

The book... itself... of itself... by itself...
stands as a tour-de-force ...a (magnum opus)...
pages upon pages of unlimited riches and truths and
how to achieve life in abundance was never consulted.

To the thief of unbelief, I say "If there is a next time...
Break in upon the treasure of unlimited truth of self control.

Break in upon the source of abiding peace and joy.
Break in upon the discovery of love, forgiveness, and glory.
Break in upon the conduct of character.
Break in upon the book of riches of everlasting life.
Break in upon a city called New Jerusalem where the streets are made of solid gold.
Break in upon a city where the walls are made of jasper, whose foundation is of sapphire, topaz, amethyst, jacinth and sardonyx."

"Break in upon a city whose twelve gates are made of pearls. Break in upon a city that has no need of the sun, neither the moon, for it is illuminated by the Glory of God and the Lamb is the light," Revelations Ch. 21.

"And God shall wipe away all tears from their eyes; and there shall be no more death, neither sorrow, nor crying, neither shall there be any more pain: for the former things are passed away," (Revelations 21:4).

"And He showed me a pure river of water of life, clear as crystal, proceeding out of the throne of God and of the Lamb. In the midst of the street of it, and on either side of the river, was there the tree of life, which bare twelve *manner* of fruits, and yielded her fruit every month: and the leaves of the tree *were* for he healing of the nations," (Revelations 22:1-2).

God created all this for those whose names are written in the Lamb's Book of Life.

STRUGGLING THROUGH YOUR FIELD OF DISILLUSION

Strut, strut through the deepest, darkest glares of the valley
can easily make the field of life a giant disillusion.

If you see this as a hindrance... maybe your strut is not
working. Try another walk. Try a different walk.

If a different walk doesn't work... maybe you need to change
Fields, the ground you are walking on.

Something is still not working after changing your walk and
field; try walking with Jesus. He will give you a new talk
of grace through a Heavenly Field filled with purpose,
beaming with the fruits of righteousness, expectation and joy.
As you and He walk... stop by so that we may tag along.

A DAY AT THE MALL

Could not sleep –
awake all night –
dreaming of Dreston –
with garments creaming! "Buy me."
"I only cost a days 'wages.
Who cares if I'm made of Synthetic Polyester?
Who cares if I'm worm only once?
Who cares if I consist of one yard?
Who cares if my style only last one season?
I only saw one smoky club;
yet here I stand in your closet after twenty years.
I have fifty more polyesters who like me only
saw one premiere and was good for two days
wages. Over a period of twenty years
that's only about $$$$$$$$$$$$$$$$$$$$$$$$$$$$,
who cares?"

Reading XVII "A mind"

"I remember the days of old; I meditate on all thy works; I muse on the work of thy hands."

- Psalm 143:5

I CAN ADEQUATELY PROVE WITHIN A 24 HOUR PERIOD YOU CAN DO WITHOUT YOUR MIND.

It's mine, oh! Mind –
All my own –
My mind not thinking –
They told me I did not need one.
I did not need a mind to think.
Softly, swiftly, sweetly, discreetly, I put my mind away.
In some space –
At somewhere –
I cannot recall where I hid it.
Never mine –

They told me my arrival time to start my day would began at 6 AM. They even gave me an alarm clock to prove it. How easy was that? No mind of mine needed.

By way of television I was told breakfast would consist of milk and cereal. Everybody knows that we should start our day with protein. Who could resist that? They even told me the kind of cereal I needed to buy and where to get it. So, I'm convinced that getting rid of my mind may not have been such a bad idea after all.

Some girly magazine told me the kind of soap I simply could not do without. We girls already know how we cherish our soft delicate bodies, especially when and where it's needed the most. I'm beginning to not mine not having a mind.

A woman's fashion magazine picked the suit that I should wear to work. They told me it was flattering for my figure. I offered no resistance, be that as it may, my mind told me before I put it away, that I had no figure. By not trusting my mind, my IQ just went up 10 points and my emotional affirmation is completely off the charts.

Welcome to the face world where make-up kings and queens rein supreme. I am thoroughly convinced that when God created the face of Eve, every make-up company on planet earth sent a representative to the (Garden of Eden). Like Cherubs hovering above the face of Eve, waiting for the fall; not the fall of the year, but "The Great Fall."

"I stand at my vanity with no sanity; no mind to say what make-up I needed for the day. Suddenly, in a moment, I eyed up Ellen... you know the one with the pretty pastel cars. She seem to say, "I am the best from all the rest. Give me your flaws and you will have no cause for worry, whatsoever."

Did I hear a scream from the girl that covers (Mary Rose), Miss Elizabeth refuting that proposition? They all seem to have a greater solution. "Give us your face and in return we will give you *Luscious Lips... Charming Cheeks, a Flawless Face and eyes the opposite sex could get lost in.*" Opposite is overpowering and sex???, the jury is still out... no verdict has been rendered.

Everyone knows that a woman's hair is her glory. The Bible tells us that. "But if a woman has long hair, it is a glory to her: for her hair is given her for a covering," (1 Corinthians 11:15). When I wake up in the morning and look at my hair in the mirror, *Hallelujah* is not the first thought that comes to mind... oops, the absence of my mind.

They told me they had a solution for my hair... and they did, just around the corner and I walked out with a head full of *Luscious Romantic Original Wig.* I knew I was looking good... without any interference from the mind I so conveniently put away.

I'm driving to work in my hot pink and purple laid back convertible that the mind of the car salesman insisted went well with the color of my brown eyes and *Luscious Frosted Romantic Original Wig.* "Never mind!"

LADIES: IF YOU ARE WEARING A WIG AND SOMEONE ASK IF THAT'S YOUR HAIR... THE APPROPRIATE ANSWER IS "YES." DIDN'T YOU BUY IT WITH YOUR OWN MONEY?

Your job is a no brainer... which can be a good thing. You don't need a mind to tell you to do your job. Your job is something you do, day after day, week after week, month after month, and year after year. It's automatic, routine, habit. It can't get any simpler than that.

You don't need a mind to tell you when it's quitting time. The only thing you need to do is follow the migration of the crowd toward the time clock, at around 4:50 or so.

All day long I never consulted my mind about anything. Great! Because, I don't remember where I left it. I did not need it!"

We're told by the Medical Industry our health is our number one priority... or should be. The right diet, proper rest, exercise and the right amount of sleep each night is a healthy prescription. No mind can dispute that.

I must admit... it's pretty difficult to get your taste buds geared up for blanched bland broccoli... boneless, skinless, tasteless baked chicken breast, with a boring vinaigrette spinach salad. Normal human taste buds simply don't salivate over a head of lettuce. I have yet to have a craving for Cauliflower.

If I didn't know better... I would think billboards were divinely inspired. I don't know who invented billboards, but they are like Bible Verses. "Oh taste and see that the burgers are good," (Burger 1:1). "A French Fry a day keeps the cravings away," (French Fry 1:2). We all know that Jesus first miracle at Cana was the turning of water to wine (John 2). But, I don't drink wine ...I drink coke. I just don't think burgers, fries, and wine jell well together. The Billboard Bible has this huge burger (a one pounder) oozing with melted cheese... running down all sides. As I glide down the check out lane... my taste buds are hopping, skipping and jumping all over the place. Even my wig gets excited. My hormones rage... my senses get fired up for a *wonderful awakening.* Paul Cezanne could not have painted a prettier burger. "Dinner is final."

Someone said "If you don't mind, it doesn't matter." The absence of a mind "really" doesn't matter.

Night is slowly creeping toward a dark descent.
I don't wonder where my mind went.
I have not used it all day long.
Nothing really went drastically wrong.
Bed time is the next thing in line.
And for this... I do not need a mind.

When we were small, my grandmother would always tell us girls, ***"Keep your dress down... keep your dress down!"*** I thought she meant, when the wind increase, keep your dress down. As I became older... one day it dawned on me... keeping my dress down had nothing to do with the *"wind,"* but it had everything to do with the the *"men."* So much for Sex Education 101.

ACTUALLY, MY GRANDMOTHER'S COMPLETE QUOTE WAS, "KEEP YOUR DRAWERS UP AND KEEP YOUR DRESS DOWN."

My motto became, "Cover everything humanly possibly, and give everything impossible to the divine will of God." I operated under the assumption that a woman should leave some things to a man's imagination. After sin entered the Garden of Eden... even Eve covered the *"possible"* with fig leaves (Genesis 3:7). From that moment on, Adam had to use his imagination.

It's really not appropriate or a good idea for a married woman to go to bed wearing a negligee over her pajamas. When it's cold outside, ladies, let your Adam turn up the thermostat on the inside.

It's all in a 24 hour day, without the interference of your mind telling you what to do.

When you can master one day without your mind getting in the way, the rest becomes sheer instinct... and you can brag to your friends about the amazing minds of others.

Reading XVIII "Marriage"

"O magnify the Lord with me, and let us exalt His name together."

- Psalm 34:3

If your marriage is on the rocks it could be due to something as simple as a lack of exercise. An increase in blood flow and oxygen to the brain can work wonders.

Marriage is a loaded word; so, add to the load... gracefully.

If you think about marriage long enough it may make sense or it may not make sense.

Marriage is not a word to dread unless you are void of energy.

I know that marriage can work because God ordained it to do just that.

Some newly weds wish they knew more about marriage. Some who've been married 50 years wish they knew less about marriage.

When two people get married their laughter should increase 100%, if it doesn't, then, they need to stop buying lemons.

Men! Don't marry a woman who doesn't like poetry and wisdom... Psalms, Proverbs, Ecclesiastes, Job.

Some women object to men not helping around the house or not listening or communicating with them, but the highest form of neglect for a married woman is her husband not giving her the attention and admiration as he did when they were dating. So, DATE HER.

Marriage is something you make happen or you don't make happen. If marriage made itself happen then you would be unnecessary.

I believe there is such a thing as marriages made in Heaven... I just don't know any.

A woman is like a dictionary... you read a dictionary to find meanings for words. You read a woman to examine her words.

When a woman takes her husband for granted, for him it's a heart thing. When a husband takes his wife for granted, for her it's a head thing.

Never judge how good or bad your mate is by their last performance.

God knows more about marriage than anyone I know, so, why not let Him be your analyst and guide?

The only ones on earth who know whether their marriage is good or bad are the husband and wife, so, consult each other.

If you believe your marriage will never get better, then, you operate under the right belief system.

If you believe your marriage will get better with your continuous effort, then, you operate under the right belief system.

If time could heal a bad marriage, time would be a great antidote for healing and God and miracles are unnecessary.

A married woman once told me that certain aspects of marriage were just too intimate. It was then I knew that the intimate aspects of marriage were created by God. Love is the seed for intimacy... where all aspects are permitted.

I believe a good marriage is the healthiest and greatest relationship two people can have on earth... definitely something to be in pursuit of... the greatest show on earth.

When Adam saw Eve he said "Yes." This is why yes is such an obstinate word.

Men! If God gave Adam a wife... it could be his idea to give you one.

A woman is a responsibility waiting for a sponsor.

A woman may not necessarily become a wife after she says "I do."
A woman may become a wife when she decides to. A man marries
a woman and she becomes his wife at some point in the marriage,
hopefully sooner than later.

At what point after the marriage ceremony can a man know that he
has a wife... when she decides she doesn't need to think about it.

Some believe that "I DO" is just for the marriage ceremony only
and some think "I DON'T" is for life after the marriage ceremony.

If marriage between a man and a woman was not God's idea, then
whose idea was it?

Single people are not married because they didn't say I do. They
are not married because they refuse to say I do and not mean it.

Men! How can you know she is truly a wife? Some believe,
somewhere along the road of divine intervention.

Some women decide to become wives before the marriage
ceremony. Some women decide to become wives during the
ceremony. Some women decide to become wives after the marriage
ceremony. Some women are caught in a dilemma of what to be.

Men! If the woman you married has not yet become your wife,
then, you have not yet figured out her game plan.

At the time of the marriage ceremony, "*I do*" is automatically
anticipated. After the ceremony, "*I do*" can become an observed
delusion.

When a man marries a woman the greatest thing he can do is
develop a six sense, or she will give him one. It's called "The
Female Sense."

Marriage is not just an 8 letter word. Divorce is not just a 7 letter word. There is a higher priority in the numbering system.

When a wife says "I have a headache... I don't feel good," "**men**, thank God for a greater opportunity He has accorded you... **THERAPY!**"

If we spend all our time trying to figure out marriage we may never have one.

The perfect marriage is between a robot and a human... if the human program the robot right.

If you had a perfect marriage God would be unnecessary.

A woman is made up of many parts... the part you notice first may be your greatest discovery or your least discovery.

I love four letter words... love, life, give, date, kiss, talk, hear, look, food, book, body, more, baby, lamb, Mark, Luke, John, seek, find, Mike, good.

Some women want to be chased. Some women want to be caught. Count up the mileage... you may need new tires.

Marriage is like a bank... you make a deposit... you get a return... no deposit... no return.

Intimacy has a lot to do with attitude. A postulating before the bedroom, in the bedroom and after the bedroom.

Men! Marry a caregiver... just make sure you can distinguish between a nurse... a wife... a mother.

Men! Women have something I call "<u>**An Unspoken Grading System,**</u>" it may not always be fair, it may not always be unfair, but I don't think it is based on what men do or don't do so much as to why they do what they do.

Marriage will not always make sense. Clay and spittle placed on the eyes of the blind man by Jesus didn't make sense either, but once the instruction was activated it **WORKED** (John 9:6-7).

In the beginning Adam and Eve saw each other through the eyes of God... no arguing... no fussing... no fighting. After sin entered the "Human Race," they saw each other through human eyes.

MARRIAGE IS ABOUT ALWAYS FINDING WAYS TO FORGIVE.

Married couples should always be mindful of everyday small things. Small can be magnified a thousand times when neglected or taken for granted.

Think of your spouse as a treasure... a gift from God and treat him/her as such. How would you treat the president if he came for a visit? Think of your spouse as on a 50 year mission from God.

The word for love is "**ENDLESS.**"

Divorce happens when marriage is self-taught instead of God-taught.

Marriage should not be decided... it should be discovered. Sometimes it is hard to decide. Discovery is something new that has been learned or found... a potential journey for great success.

Women, is there a hierarchy in the lower animal kingdom? Is there a hierarchy in the plant kingdom? Is there a hierarchy in the upper animal kingdom? Is there a hierarchy in your home? You may consult Biology for some answers, but the Bible is our best source for all the answers.

Women! If you don't believe you married a great guy, then, you didn't.

Sometimes two in the kitchen is just as important as two in the bedroom. This does not necessitate that both need to do the cooking. It's called "**KITCHEN TALK**"

Your treatment of your mate is your perception of him/her after twenty years of marriage.

Women! Godly men want to protect their ideals, their assignment, their ideas and aspirations, their marriages, their families, their solitude, their limitations, themselves.

Women! You may not have married an Abraham, Isaiah, Jacob Joseph, David, Elijah, Jeremiah, Matthew, Mark, Luke or John, but does he know any of these men?

Men! Her name may not be Esther, Abigail, Ruth or Rebecca, but does she know anyone in the Bible by those names?

During the dating process they could not keep their hands off each other. After the marriage process they can't seem to put their hands on each other. There is a reason for both!!!

When in the same room, if at all possible, spouses should always face each other when engaged in conversation, a healthy gesture of interest and respect.

You may have heard the expression "action speak louder than words." You may create an encyclopedia on "the interpretation of silence." Some tend to believe 90% of all communication is non-verbal.

Disagreements in marriages should be kept civil... just keep in mind that the Bible is always right and somebody may be wrong.

The way your mate fantasizes about you is the way he, she will treat you.

Saint John of the Cross states that "**The evening of life will be judged on love alone.**" I believe marriages should be judged on love all day long. Read "**Ephesians 5.**" "**The Book of Saints by** Jo Rose."

Ladies! You may not go around your house all day long calling him **Lord,** simply, because his name is not **Abraham** and he may not go around the house all day long with a rod in his hand trying to part the waters in the swimming pool, because his name is not Moses. But, if any of the above happens; don't let it mess with your mind. There are people on earth who call their earthly counterparts (Thou Most Holy Father) and no one ever freaks. Anyone can suffer an illusion or learn magic.

When was the last time your marriage had a good laugh? That may be too long.

The thermostat is not broken... the heating unit is working just fine... the refrigerator is in the kitchen, so, why is it so cold in the bedroom?

Marriage is only as good or as bad as you desire it to be.

Are you and your mate sleeping in a king size bed with a single bed mindset? The large space between the two of you may not go unoccupied.

Does the path to the bedroom seem like the same path to citizenship? **EARNED...**

She would "**love, honor** and **obey**... did she say... **IF?**"

You were dating for a year... you got married, but your husband didn't sleep with you on your wedding night... was that the first time he didn't sleep with you?

Marriage should not only be a meeting of the minds, but a meeting of the bodies as well.

If your mate doesn't seem to be the person you married, remember, there may be more than one of them. The others may have finally showed up. So, don't try to guess how many are coming to dinner, just make sure you have enough place settings for everyone... and hope they don't all show wearing the same outfits... it could get down right confusing.

Are you married... sleeping single... living single... thinking single... acting single... who are you?

The marriage license has been unseen, hidden away for 20 years. The lines of demarcation have been clearly drawn throughout the house... throughout the minds... throughout the bodies... the only reluctance seem to lie in the splitting of the assets.

If your regret about your marriage is that you married the wrong person, then, someone may very well have... could it possibly happen again?

Not knowing something that you need to know doesn't make it okay, neither does justification without exploration make it okay either.

Lady! You are married to a man of God... not a "god" of God.

Have your marriage reached the expiration date? "Til' death do us part."

Ladies! Nuts are a good food source, but you don't have to marry one.

Is your marriage more like a comma... a period... a colon... a semicolon or a question mark?

Some women want to be the wife of a man.

Some women want to be the wife of a husband.
Some women want to be the wife of both.

Women! You don't need to swing from a chandelier or glide down a Pole, you can create ten thousand experiences by being earth bound.

Women! You have not found husbands because finding a husband was never your responsibility or assignment. "Whoso findeth a wife findeth a good thing, and obtaineth favor of the Lord." (Proverbs 18:22).

Men! The one not taken may have been the path of least resistance.

If your marriage is stuck in neutral it's not time for you to change wives. It's time for you to discover that there is another gear... how about drive.

In order for marriage to remain interesting one must maintain interest.

Ladies! The one you stood with at the wedding altar that said "I do," may not be the same one you took home after the wedding ceremony that didn't say anything.

Ladies! You may not know who you are living with. The whereabouts of your real husband may never be revealed.

Men! you will never know a woman the way a woman knows a woman. We have more movements than a symphony. Only we can interpret each movement, but not fully!!!

Women! Do you wear life well or does life wear you?

Her kisses may not curl your toe-nails... the bedroom activity may not send your hormones raging. The cooking in the kitchen may remind you of 4 week old spoils. "Is this due to a lack of passion... OR?"

Men! Don't let your eyes be your guide. At some point down the road gravity and hormones will take over her anatomical body parts and they will travel South and just maybe East and West. You may not end up the way you started out either!!!

Is your mate predominately a left brain thinker... a right brain thinker... a whole brain thinker or none of the above?

She had a beautiful, elaborate wedding ceremony... she even said, "*I do*," but she forgot to get married. *I do*, was from the lips only. But, an *I don't*, was from the heart.

A married man enters to discover, seek pleasure, to explore, for satisfaction, to satisfy, to give pleasure... and!

A married woman receives to give access, to get love, seek approval, for hope, to get a reward, keep harmony, through obligation, a sense of duty.

She said "Marriage seems like a bond ...a bonding like Elmer's Glue... like Cement Glue." "Maybe, that's why the divorce, the splitting, the splitting apart destroys the contents."

She said "I committed the crime of marriage... I served my sentence of 25 years... my divorce decree will be final tomorrow... I will be **FREE**."

Are you **HAPPILY** married... **HAPPY** to be married, or just **HAPPEN** to be married?

She said "Marriage would not seem so final if I didn't have to think about I am."

The goal of marriage should become a habit... a lifetime habit.

When you think of your mate it should remind you of just how wonderfully generous God is.

Many spend more time on preparing for the wedding and less time on preparing for the marriage. A wedding is for a day... A marriage is for a lifetime.

Married couples should start each day with a *smile*, a *kiss, I love you* and a *prayer.*

Marriage is really about **3** things... **WANTS... NEEDS...** and **EXPECTATIONS.**
A successful marriage is about **ALWAYS THINKING** of the **NEEDS, WANTS AND EXPECTATIONS OF YOUR SPOUSE FIRST.**
A happy marriage is about **GIVING** and **TAKING.**
A **marriage** that will stand the test of time is about... **STRIKING A COMMON MEDIUM.**

She stated, "Sometimes I feel like giving my husband a piece of my mind." My reply, "Just make sure you don't give him the best piece of your mind... you're going to need the best piece for the rest of your life."

If your marriage has run out of steam... someone needs to build a new fire (rekindle the flames baby).

You think your wife has passed "the flower of her youth"... flowers die... buy her some fresh flowers.

I am of the opinion the word never should not be used in marriage... whether in a connotation of good or bad. Only God will never leave us or forsake us (Hebrews 13:5).

While dating he promised you the world... the moon... the stars. After marriage you only got an apartment. The moon, stars and the world were never his to give. God has no objection to him buying land and building houses.

We can laugh without purpose... we can cry without purpose. We should never speak without purpose, it could be injurious.

When it comes to marriage knowing something and seeing something may not always be so obvious.

After 30 years of marriage she is not as firm... her moves are no longer earth shaking... there's extra skin under her chin... her dove eyes have become deer eyes... just remember... you have a new life. Is there anything wrong with new?

If your husband insists on you getting a job outside the home... and also insist on you during all the house work, cleaning, cooking, laundry, raising the children, and other duties, you need to draw up a *prenuptial agreement.* It should state "If you give birth to the first child, I will give birth to the second child."

"A child is an innocent unspoiled mind waiting to become the persuaded opinions of others."

Would you rather spend **3** hours in the **Kitchen** or **3** hours in the **Emergency Room**?

What you eat can directly affect how you perform in your marriage... in your life.

As a hot cup of tea on a cold night with a warm fire is soothing to the body... a good wife is as soothing to her husband's soul.

Dull knives in the kitchen won't cut it... neither will dull marriages!

What you put in your stomach (food) should be more expensive than what you put on your body (clothes). It may be a little more expensive to shop at organic markets, but your body was designed to last a lifetime. Your clothes are designed to last for a season.

Some of the same cooking spices in your food cabinet just might possibly spice up your marriage also.

A healthy daily diet is one of the most nutritional, rewarding and considerate thing a wife can do for her husband and family. "Savor the rewards." "Beloved, I wish above all things that thou mayest prosper and be in **health**, even as thy soul prosper," (3 John 1:2).

Husbands/Wives! You don't just have to be married everyday... you can get married everyday. Marriage is about the 3 C'S... Commitment, Ceremony and Celebration. You don't have to wait 20 years to renew your marriage vows. You can renew them every year... as often as you like. After twenty years you may have forgotten what they were and not quite lived up to them. The ceremony can be in the bath tub, on the beach, in the closet or anyplace you choose. Creativity is the water that moves the boat.

We will never know all we need to know about something we need to know about.

She asked, "After the 'Garden of Eden' was sex a punishment for Eve and a pleasure for Adam?" It may depend on whose passion prevailed first. The answer may seem inconsequential or the question.

In matters of marriage, "Should the heart speak louder than the head?"

Laugh **often... love always... give generously... pray much... listen well... make making love a priority... be happy... stay healthy... gain wisdom... be a Godly Servant... use discipline and restraint. Give, give, give... unconditional.**

"HAVE A GODLY MARRIAGE"

Reading XIX "Genius (VS) Mad Genius"

"Whoso is wise, and will observe these things, even they shall understand the loving-kindness of the Lord."

- Psalm 107:43

GENIUS (VS) MAD-GENIUS

"MY OBSERVATION"

STAYING IN THE CONTEXT OF A CERTAIN PERIMETER

Genius is a straight line where Alpha and Omega draw their distance.

Mad-Genius is a straight line until Alpha and Omega decide to meet between the line, forgetting their distance.

Genius has its place.

Mad-Genius can't seem to find its place.

Genius is a point of recognition of something needing to be.

Mad-Genius is not being able to distinguish the separation.

Genius is marching around the walls and blowing a horn.

Mad-Genius is standing from afar shouting "No, no, no, that won't work."

Genius is innately identifying Black, White, Brown, Yellow and Red.

Mad-Genius is trying to get rid of one or some.

Genius is writing 100 books and knowing that 100 is the number of books you have written and not the title of any.

Mad-Genius is not being able to distinguish the title from the number.

Genius is not being mad about not being a mad-genius.

Mad-Genius is being mad about not being a genius.

Genius is discovering your difference and making a difference.

Mad-Genius is teetering on the brink of both.

Genius is not categorized by numbers – not counting the times you took out the trash or the times you fell.

Mad-Genius is counting the times you took out the trash and counting the times you fell.

Genius is Joshua and Caleb seeing farther than the 10 spies because their faith was standing on the shoulders of God.

Mad-Genius is the 10 spy's faith standing on the shoulders of the giants.

Genius knows God has already planted His DNA in us for greatness.

Mad-Genius is saying "I don't know how to activate it."

Genius is down home cooking where you burn the grits and formulate a new recipe.

Mad-Genius is him yelling "you always burn the grits." "(It's a new recipe-stupid)."

Genius is flawed, knowing that in spite of it you can begin again.

Mad-Genius is not knowing you are flawed and staying who you are.

Genius is you seeing you the way God sees you.

Mad-Genius is you seeing you the way others see you (mad, mad, mad).

Genius is stamped across the mind of what can be.

Mad-Genius is a stamped conscious of what can never be.

Genius is tampering with the broken until you get it right.

Mad-Genius is blaming the manufacture for not making it perfect.

Genius is a bad day making ready for a great tomorrow.

Mad-Genius is a bad day and expecting the same tomorrow.

Genius is you at the end of your rope... tying a knot and hanging on (Peter).

Mad-Genius is being at the end of your rope and commence to hang yourself (Judas).

Genius knows the process is never complete.

Mad-Genius is thinking you have arrived... when you know you have not.

Genius is staring into the mirror and seeing the potential for greatness.

Mad-Genius is staring into the mirror and seeing no possibilities.

Genius said "I'm single."

Mad-Genius says "And you always will be."

Genius got married.

Mad-Genius said "It will never last."

Genius had children.

Mad-Genius said "They will never amount to anything."

Genius says "I have a wisdom problem."

Mad-Genius says "Get rid of one or the other."

Genius said "I'm getting old."

Mad-Genius said "Cheer up... most of your bad days are behind you. You only have a few more bad days left."

Genius says "My health is not what it once was."

Mad-Genius said "And nothing else about you is what it once was."

Genius turned into mad-genius... ripped up the painting and cut off his ear.

Genius wrote a best seller.

Mad-Genius went out and shot himself.

Genius knows God puts the genius in us.

Mad-Genius is us failing to recognize the Godliness.

The satisfaction of a genius is never satisfied.

Genius is searching longer and harder for more than is necessary, because there is no expiration date on the need to search.

Genius speaks loudest when there is no audience.

If you need to verbally affirm your genius... then, someone else may verbally affirm that you are not.

Are you waiting for genius to turn up at your door... wait no more... it is already inside.

There are 5 AM geniuses... 10 PM geniuses and there are 24 hour, all day long geniuses... which are you?

If you think you are a left over genius from another century... connect the dots. . . !

Why do we need to imagine ourselves as being genius when God has already put genius in us.

Genius is the awareness that we did not create the stars, but did we have the wisdom to reach for them?

If I had not been created by my creator with the equipment to be genius ... I would never know I could be ...I am.

A mad-genius was living on the streets in a ghetto ...when one day a genius came by and asked him, "why are you living like this?" "The man in the ghetto stated, "I never knew I was a genius."

You can be and not know... you can know and not be...

Have you ever been in the company of 3, 4 and 5 year olds and felt you were in the company of genius? You may very well have been.

Genius is lying dormant in us waiting for a wake-up-call.

Genius is inspiration with feet taking you where you need to go.

Genius is traveling down the path of great resistant, but ending up on a road paved with no resistant.

The right time for genius is always.

Your greatest desire may not necessarily be to attain the status of a genius, but if you keep doing great things... genius may show up anyway...

Marie Curie, Dr. George Washington Carver, Helen Keller, Thomas Edison, Dr. Martin Luther King, Frederick Douglass, John Keats, Richard N. Wright.

Genius is not the highest standard, but the higher standard is genius.

Most geniuses don't know that they are!

Your genius may be like the grading system of a "boxer" in the ring... *light weight... middle weight... heavy weight.*

Genius knows who wakes them us in the morning.

Mad-Genius mind is stuck in a dilemma of questioning.

Genius places a high priority on listening and learning.

Mad-Genius places a higher priority on talking.

Genius recognizes the superfluous in life and tries to take heed.

Mad-Genius is keeping up the pace unnecessarily.

So, can we *rightly say* we all contain Genius and Mad-Genius? *Justly so*!

Thomas Alva Edison states, "*Genius is one percent inspiration and ninety-nine percent perspiration.*"

Some facts about Edison's life:
- He left school at the age of 12 due to an increasing hearing problem.
- Some thought he was retarded. Eventually, he became completely deaf.
- He questioned everything!!!

- He refused to accept that impossibilities could not become facts without relentless experimentation and results which convinced him to the contrary.
- He was the most prolific inventor ever known.
- He jointly and singularly is accredited with 1093 patents. He filled a patent every 2 weeks for 83 years.

Some quotes by Edison:

"I find out what the world needs, then I go ahead and try to invent it."

"We don't know one millionth of one percent of anything."

Source: Science, "**100 Scientist who changed the world**," (Jo Balchin).

"I believe Genius stems from the ability to persevere."

AUNT NIG

She was analogous to a "King James Bible Verse,"
never changing.
She never felt a need to transform her habits.
Everyday remained the same...

I remember her unwillingness
to enlist our next generation, century, to change out her
wood burning cook stove;
to modify her light bulb fixture on a string hanging
from her ceiling would have been a "Cardinal Sin."
Everyday remained the same.

On her back porch for six decades... rusting... hung a
#3 ten tub on a nail...
replicating from a washing machine to a bath pot.
Everyday remained the same.

With one slight twist of the wrist... on a serious chicken
day, Aunt Nig would separate a chicken's head
from the body quicker than flash lightening.
Everyday remained the same.

If any creature crawled, slithered, laid, played, hesitated,
hovered, stopped or hopped near her egg nest they would
suffer severe hack damage or even death.
Everyday remained the same.

In the early days a water-well stood on the West side of her
Dog-Trot-House. On a summer day we could see our silhouette
as we yanked up a dipper of cool sipping water.

When asked how she was feeling... her reply was always, "I
ant no good." As she picked out the painful body parts,
nearing her last days she proclaimed, "I ant a bitter good,
everything hurts."
Everyday remained the same.

Aunt Nig transcended the other day.
That little Dog-Trot-House is declared a "City Landmark."

Her little antique bowls were passed around.
Many hand-stitched blankets were dispatched... as we folded
our grieving banners and headed back to the business of living.
And, almost nothing remains the same.

Reading XX "Hospitalizing"

"Cast thy burden upon the Lord, and He shall sustain thee: He shall never suffer the righteous to be moved."

- Psalm 55:22

Demoralizing on hospital bed I loll, that day, without a hint
of what it meant, damaged and disordered, broken and bewildered,
my eyes fluttered as someone uttered, only the doctors, not to
shutter.
With white robe and clean nose, entered they, with a wave, that
said hello. Prying and prodding, began they, as they made their way,
not a pretty sight, but there I loll.

Stethoscopes soared from pockets of prestige to land on my
chest that told of all the rest, answers I needed as they
proceeded and told of horror and hell that day. A rushing
car came crushing my body, strewn across the road
I shatter; I understood some did pray, not a pleasing sight,
but there I loll.

Down and dazed, I slightly raised to hear as doctors came near.
They told of broken bones not shattered by stones, but by a
man and a car that failed to stop, Tibia Plateau, was attributed
to a badly broken knee, you see. Compound Fracture on Femur,
I was not dreaming. Leg Cast and pens protruded from end to end.
Not very attractive, but there I loll.

Pain began to bind in the darkest recesses of my mind.
I knew I had little time to hurry, not worry, and get dope,
without, there was no hope. The nurse injected whatever, the
fix came quick, as I loll.

A new day approached, water, tea and thin soup, no
breakfast food stuck in my throat. A sensation commence to tell
me I was about to float. I sent a little emergency note. Miss Nurse
came quickly, this was an understood mission. Something steel,
cold and looking old holstered my behind, bedpan bound and
unwillingly, I loll.

Holidays came and holidays went... all my days were well nigh
spent.

Visitors came, and visitors went leaving me virtually helpless as they mete out good bys. Bingo prowlers were on the make, boards soared, tempers flowed around dollar sweet perfume and ewer of dollop, but sticky stole the show. Just as pretty as I pleased, I loll.

Rain lugged pain, quaint stories told very bold of rainy days predicting crazy ways. From aching bones came loud mourns. All night long I sing my song "Help, Help" not one so sweetly tuned in June. Gleams of lightening collided with beams and put a damper on patients sleep and dreams. Once again, screaming Loudly, I loll

Jacketing two thirds of me, this new cast creating such a mass, I felt no less like a mummy, well, more like a dressmaker's dummy. To scratch this itch, hitch this twitch... somebody give me please, an elongated coat-hanger, zigzag kind. Awfully and lawfully I needed the urge to stop this surge.
With an itinerant mind due to months
of hospital slump, several up to now, some relief, but let it be, silently, I loll.

Books, newspapers, magazines and crafts, I was good to go from day to day, laying on my gurney, sprawled in the hall, seen by all; shooting the breeze with veterans of ease, opening up cans of sardines that sometimes smell from hospitalized kitchens. They were straight back from Nam, Viet that is, and stories told of addictions, missing limbs, altered minds and everything else of the kind, in view of the fact, I loll.

Doctors did all to help these war boys. Their sleep meds consisted of a miller... beer that is, carefully concealed in brown paper bags. Being told, I approached my doctor with bold, millers began to show up at my bedside late at night. No way was I to drink, only to be in the wink, but this I knew, as yet I loll.

Christmas gloomed, the horizon loomed like hot plate on high noon burning my stew. Visitors imparted holiday cheer. Brazing Carolers nip the nippy on Christmas Eve. No presents requested, only

needed I a hi, good-by, see you later, merry, merry and doctors
to tell me the day I no longer had to loll.

Teensy, weensy bits of shaking, earthquake in the making.
Rumbling, tumbling order of the day... patients gasping
and grabbing, no sleeping, only weeping on this California
January - Day. The Rector Scale predicted widespread damage
and hospital panic. Hospital fractures showed all the action,
cracks and crevices made for big devices. Hitherto, I loll.

Last leg of my stay, about to be sent away,
on a round table I lay, therapy being the order of the day.
A mechanical lift strapped and all prevented even a fall.
It elevated by body until I stood tall. Through pain
came gain, with grief, relief. A new tune in June lifted
me to my feet, matters settled, there I stood.

SOME HISTORY:

MATTHEW JOSEPH THADDEUS STEPANEK

Matthew Joseph Thaddeus Stepanek, better known as (Mattie) was born July 17, 1990. He passed away in 2004 at the ripe your age of 13 yrs. Despite being born with Dysautonomic Mitochondrial Myopathy, a genetic Neuromuscular Disease that weakened his muscles and caused difficulty in breathing and lack of control over bodily functions, none of these hindered him from fulfilling his assigned destiny.

He was a peacemaker. He wrote 5 volumes of poetry about peace; of which all made the "New York Times Best Seller List."

After seeing him on "The Oprah Show," I was captivated by this young genius.

Oprah called him, "An Inspiration." Miss Maya Angelou, who wrote the introduction to one of his books, referred to him as, "A Kindred Spirit" and "Fellow Poet."

President Jimmy Carter and Mattie became friends. President Carter described Mattie as "The Most Remarkable Person He Had Ever Known." President Jimmy Carter and Oprah also attended Mattie's Home-Going.

"Many have done more with less time... many have done less with more time."

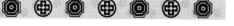

A POEM FOR MATTIE

"IN PURSUIT OF PEACE"

Someone stated "Peace is the absence of war," others
write books "War and Peace." Webster says, "peace: a-
Freedom from civil disturbance 1: a state of tranquility or quiet:
a: harmony in personal relations 4: a state or period of mutual
concern between governments b: a pack or agreement to end
hostilities."

A little boy penned best selling poems about peace,
whose small frail flesh knew only pain that never ceased.

He embarked upon his God given mission;
established his blessed position.

His thinking and writing was far beyond his 13 years.
He spoke... people cried and cheered.
Peace must generate in the spirit of individuals.

His hand wrote what his heart spoke.

The spirit of peace must put the flesh of war under
subjection.

The wildness of the flesh wants confrontation.
The quietness of the spirit yearn meditation.

The stupidity of the flesh cries out for power.
The wisdom of the spirit-mission is for peace.

The torment of the flesh lashes out... revenge without end!
The conscious of the spirit ask "after revenge... what then?"

The flesh is angry and stirred!
The spirit yearns to be heard!

"He that is slow to anger is better than the mighty;
and he that ruleth his spirit than he that taketh a city,"
(Proverbs 16:32).

(1 Corinthians 1:29) "That no flesh should glory in His presence."

"For all flesh is as grass, and all the glory of man as the flower of
grass. The grass withereth, and the flower thereof falleth away,"
(1 Peter 1:24.).

"Therefore, brethren, we are debtors, not to the flesh, to live
after the flesh," (Romans 8:12).

"For if ye live after the flesh, ye shall die: but if ye through
the Spirit do modify the deeds of the body, ye shall live,"
(Romans 8:13)

"For they that are after the flesh do mind the things of the flesh;
but they that are after the Spirit the things of the Spirit,"
(Romans 8:5).

While his frail flesh was dying daily, his Spirit constantly
renewed itself like the budding of fresh spring flowers under
tiny falcate raindrops.

The Spirit used a child body to prick the hearts of thousands
untold. His genesis started with a dark well of uncertainty,
but the Spirit motivated the body with an urgency to be heard.

As he appropriately proceeded to his decided post,
I doubt not that his poems are being enjoyed by the
"Angelic Host."

HER CHILDHOOD YEARS

Never mine a small Louisiana town that barely bothered to dot the page of the state map. Never mine the gripping reality of poverty interfering upon the barren countryside like old wild tree branches clawing in every direction.

Never mine a life where tall stood small, where there were no dreams to dream... where hope disguised itself under a thick inscription of skepticism. Human minds were lowered, captured and locked in smokehouses like high hanging beef parts.

A woman was forbidden to cross the road to dare... she simply remained over the line of hopeless despair. Where, the words, may I, should I, can I, never stamped the human thought. The eye of the child and the eye of the adult never told of an every day meeting.

The backdrop of absurdity loomed like painted clouds crowding the canvas of Claude Monet. A symbolism of quarantine kept love and joy at bay. Great expectations rose to the height of one small pancake.

House rules stood refute to the first amendment rights of freedom of speech. Recipes of canning were gathered from fruit trees. Setting hens gleefully spread around their protein... fried, baked, boiled, scrambled, in soups and holiday dressings.

Almanacs dictated moons, rains, suns, seasons and times for crop planting. Pot-belly black wash pots stole the dingy linen, repented and returned them back lily white.

A MOTHER

Her love for children and especially the nurturing and caring for babies brought her great joy.

Her love for learning and education was evident. She returned to night school while we were still in high school to get her diploma.

she would read advertisement papers as if they were Unabridged Encyclopedias or dictionaries. She often denied herself things she needed, to purchase books for her children. She knew some of us love learning.

She loved voting and would study the voting ballot as if she would be tested and graded. When she didn't understand something, she would ask someone.

Etched in my memory are the home medical non-prescription treatments.
They consisted of Watkins Liniments, Vicks Salves, for colds and flu.
They made home concoctions such as Mullen Tea, Cow Chip Tea, Corn Chuck Tea; no doubt, handed down from generations.

Those Grey Eyes for a woman of color were given back to brilliance.
Those Brown Indian Fringed Slippers provided miles of good ware.
That White Stained Apron gave up specialized family recipes, retired.
Those Healing Hands over my sick chest folded in rest.

She left her little Home without defrosting the ice box.
Her Easy Rocker stood empty without getting that last screech.
Her Pink Dove (soap) reclined peacefully on her bathroom sink.
Memories of her awareness stood near her closet door.

A drop of rain miasma her windowpane.
Her silence of Radio Gospel Programs lingered.
Her Water Well Pump offered no drink.
Her Unspoken Words were ever fervent.

Her birthday four days before was a final farewell.
Early on a Monday morning she hesitated not to stay.
There was a getting together of just she and they,
as she gave her last smile and entered the next stage.

MISS MAYA ANGELOU

I was blessed to be in the presence of Miss Maya Angelou on two separate occasions. I first heard her speak at the University of Southern California, where I was a student, in the late seventies. I was privileged to be in her presence for the last time in 2011, where she once again stimulated my brain at a Barnes & Noble Bookseller. The following poem encompasses some of her many words and memories.

MISS MAYA ANGELOU (1928-2014)

The sound of her voice
rang like England's "Big Ben."
The choices of her spoken words
were as the gleaning of first fruits.
The ears of her audiences
drank in her poetry, her songs,
like a thirsty virgin stream.
She spoke without script, but her
audience seem to know they were
being taken on a wonderful trip.
We sat and listen without making
a sound... completely spellbound.
A lady of elegance.
A lady of grace.
A lady who pioneered and paved paths
so others could travel through.
Her strut was with pride.
She smiled with style.
She sowed her genius around college campuses,
universities, schools, and a presidential
inauguration; like a farmer sewing seed in the
soil, anticipating an outstanding harvest.
The lady knew why "The Caged Bird Sings."
She knew how to "Prepare Great Food All Day
Long."
The lady set, "Hallelujah! The Welcome Table."
The lady told "The Heart of a Woman."
She wrote children's books.
The lady said "All God's Children Need Traveling
Shoes."
The lady stated, "Wouldn't Take Nothing for My
Journey Now."
The lady wrote "Just Give Me a Cool Drink of
Water 'fore I Diiie."

"The Phenomenal Woman," and many, many other works of wisdom Miss Angelou gave us have blessed our lives, and her works will continue to uplift and educate us as we journey up this road known as life.

Her earthly pen is rested, but not before staining her many wonderful pages with her love, her journeys, her struggles, her discoveries, her experiences and her life.

Printed in the United States
By Bookmasters